1. THE AUTOBIOGRAPHY OF AN UNKNOWN SOUTH AFRICAN, by Naboth Mokgatle (1971)

2. MODERNIZING RACIAL DOMINATION: *South Africa's Political Dynamics,* by Heribert Adam (1971)

3. THE RISE OF AFRICAN NATIONALISM IN SOUTH AFRICA: *The African National Congress, 1912-1952,* by Peter Walshe (1971)

4. TALES FROM SOUTHERN AFRICA, by A. C. Jordan (1973)

5. LESOTHO 1970: *An African Coup Under the Microscope,* by B. M. Khaketla (1972)

6. TOWARDS AN AFRICAN LITERATURE: *The Emergence of Literary Form in Xhosa,* by A. C. Jordan (1972)

7. LAW, ORDER, AND LIBERTY IN SOUTH AFRICA, by A. S. Mathews (1972)

8. SWAZILAND: *The Dynamics of Political Modernization,* by Christian P. Potholm (1972)

9. THE SOUTH WEST AFRICA/NAMIBIA DISPUTE: *Documents and Scholarly Writings on the Controversy Between South Africa and the United Nations,* by John Dugard (1973)

10. CONFRONTATION AND ACCOMMODATION IN SOUTHERN AFRICA: *The Limits of Independence,* by Kenneth W. Grundy (1973)

11. POWER, APARTHEID, AND THE AFRIKANER CIVIL RELIGION, by Thomas D. Moodie (1973)

12. JUSTICE IN SOUTH AFRICA, by Albie Sachs (1973)

13. AFRIKANER POLITICS IN SOUTH AFRICA, 1934-1948, by Newell M. Stultz (1974)

Afrikaner Politics in South Africa,
1934-1948

Afrikaner Politics in South Africa, 1934-1948

Newell M. Stultz

UNIVERSITY OF CALIFORNIA PRESS
BERKELEY / LOS ANGELES / LONDON

University of California Press
Berkeley and Los Angeles, California

University of California Press, Ltd.
London, England

ISBN: 0-520-02452-4
Library of Congress Catalog Card Number: 73-76116

Printed in the United States of America

To Betsie

Contents

Preface

My interest in South African politics began during a year of postgraduate study as a Fulbright Fellow at the University of Pretoria in 1955-1956, and later it was strengthened by marriage into a South African family. My interest in the specific topic of this work, however, was prompted by curiosity, as is doubtless the origin of most scholarly investigations. In a brief passage that is again quoted in Chapter One, Rupert Emerson stated in 1960 that the urbanization of Afrikaners in South Africa might be expected to provide increasing support in the future for "policies more in keeping with the modern world." In Chapter Nine, research findings are cited that suggest that Afrikaner urbanization may now be producing this effect, although not in South African race policy, Emerson's particular concern. In 1960, however, no such relationship was as yet apparent. On the contrary, the preceding quarter century, a period of rapid Afrikaner urbanization, was also a period of marked growth for an exclusive and often reactionary Afrikaner nationalism. I wished to find out why this was so. In particular I sought the reasons for the dramatic upset victory of Dr. D. F. Malan and the National Party over the government of Prime Minister Jan Smuts in the South African "apartheid" election of 1948. Although this is easily the most important of South African general elections, and the one that is most often recalled, scholarly treatment of it has been only cursory. Sir Keith Hancock, for example, devotes only eleven pages to the election in his 1,100 page, two-volume biography of Smuts, and no other scholar has given the election significantly more attention.

This work was prepared initially between 1962 and 1964 as a doctoral dissertation in political science at Boston University. It has been both revised and extended since then. Most of the research was conducted in South Africa under a grant from the Ford Foundation, whose generous support I gratefully acknowledge. A number of persons in both South Africa and the United States provided help and encouragement. In particular, I wish to thank Drs. Willem Kleynhans, J. J. N. Cloete, and Gwendolen M. Carter; Mr. O. A. Oosthuizen; Mr. B. J. van der Walt, MP; Senator M. P. A. Malan; and my father-in-law, Brigadier S. J. B. Olckers. I am especially indebted to my supervisors at Boston University, Professors Jeffrey Butler (now of Wesleyan University) and William J. Newman. The final writing was assisted in 1970 by a grant from the Brown University faculty summer stipend committee. Mrs. Frances Ross and Mrs. Donna Rose kindly helped with the final typing. Portions of this work appeared initially in the *Journal of Modern African Studies* and *Plural Societies* and are used here with permission. Last, I thank my wife, Betsie, who cheerfully endured endless hours of discussion of these matters. To her this work is affectionately dedicated.

I have translated into English quotations in the text that are from Afrikaans sources; and within these quotations, as in the body of the work, spelling follows American usage. Quotations in the text from English language sources, however, have not been changed with respect to spelling.

Social conflict results from the conscious
pursuit of exclusive values.

HAROLD D. LASSWELL
Encyclopaedia of the Social Sciences (1931), 4:194.

Introduction

The Union of South Africa was established on May 31, 1910, eight years to the day after the signing of the Treaty of Vereeniging that concluded the South African War (1899-1902), and its founding was the product of the cooperative efforts of men who had opposed each other in that conflict. Although the South Africa Act of 1909 that formally brought the Union into being was an enactment of the Parliament of Great Britain at Westminster, this statute was based on a draft constitution that had been prepared by a national convention that included leaders of both of the former Boer republics, and this document was subsequently ratified by each of the four South African colonies: Cape Colony, Transvaal, Orange River Colony, and Natal.[1] But despite the apparent mood of good will and compromise that attended the unification of South Africa, bitter memories of the recent struggles between Boer republicans and British imperialists throughout the last quarter of the nineteenth century were still fresh in the minds of many persons. The paramount question in 1910 was thus whether relations between Dutch-speaking and English-speaking whites in the new country would be characterized by mutual respect, tolerance, and compromise, or whether in the end one of the two language groups would succeed in dominating the other.[2]

[1]Six of the 31 delegates to the National Convention had been in the field with the republican forces during the South African War. L. M. Thompson, *The Unification of South Africa, 1902-1910* (Oxford: Clarendon Press, 1960), Appendix B.

[2]The form of government established for South Africa under the South Africa Act was substantially patterned on the Westminster

1

Indeed, this remained the principal issue in South African politics, and the chief determinant of partisan alignments from 1910 until at least 1961, when the country became a republic. After 1910 two types of political parties emerged, representing different responses to ethnic differences among whites. One type was *nationalist* in that it drew its support exclusively from one or the other of the two white language groups and stressed the traditions and the cultural, economic, and other needs of that particular group. Both pro-Boer and pro-British parties developed. But at the time of Union, Boers (or Afrikaners)[3] constituted a slight majority — 54 percent — of the South African white population, and through the years this majority gradually increased. Concurrently, the Afrikaner successfully resisted his own anglicization. A pro-British party thus had little hope of gaining power without the unlikely support of a considerable number of Afrikaners, and within a decade after 1910, most English-speaking South Africans had left the pro-British Unionist Party for a party of the second type, namely, the South African Party. This type of party was *conciliatory* in that it relegated cultural distinctions among whites to a subordinate position and sought to harmonize and reconcile the different interests within the electorate. Accordingly, such parties could hope

---

parliamentary model, but had a few unique features. Among these, the most important was a franchise that was closed to all nonwhites in the Transvaal and the Orange Free State and that discriminated *de facto* against nonwhites in both the Cape Province and Natal. Thus while Africans, Asians, and Coloureds (persons of mixed blood) together comprised nearly 80 percent of the total population at the time of the first Union census in 1911, in 1929, at the height of their influence, nonwhite voters made up only 9.2 percent of the full Union electorate. South African society is multi-ethnic, but its electoral politics has always been the nearly exclusive preserve of the two white language groups. In 1911 the population of South Africa was 5,973,394: 21.4 percent white (1,276,242); 67.3 percent African (4,019,006); 8.8 percent Coloured (525,943); and 2.5 percent Asian (152,203). Office of Census and Statistics, *Official Year Book of the Union of South Africa and of Basutoland, Bechuanaland Protectorate, and Swaziland,* No. 21 — 1940 (Pretoria: The Government Printer), pp. 123 and 1000.

[3]An Afrikaner is a white South African (or "European") who speaks Afrikaans as his home language.

to draw support from both white language groups, as nationalist parties could not. Thus from 1910 to 1960, South African politics was in general a struggle between two opposing political philosophies for the support of the Afrikaner electorate. One was Afrikaner nationalism; the other was known as "conciliation." In 1910 and again in 1934, the issue appeared to have been decided in favor of "conciliation," but in each instance a new party dedicated to the narrow and exclusive aims of Afrikaner nationalism was organized, and increased in strength until approximately fifteen years later its support among Afrikaners was sufficient to bring it to power. The purpose of this study is to explain the erosion of Afrikaner support for "conciliation" during the second of these periods. To put it more positively, we shall try to identify the reasons for the electoral revival of Afrikaner nationalism in the period leading up to the general election of 1948.

Conceptually, I have found it useful to consider white politics in South Africa from the standpoint of the *political integration* of a culturally bifurcated electorate. *Integration* is a comparatively old idea in the literature of the social sciences, and in the present period it has been widely used in studies of the "new" states. There are, however, many definitions of integration and as Aristide Zolberg has observed, "the concept wears better as a signal of topical concern than as a building block in a rigorous theoretical edifice."[4] Here integration refers to the *process* by which a society develops the *strong social cohesiveness* that allows its members to take effective action to promote common goals and mutual interests; where that collective action is political in nature — that is, where it involves the governing institutions and sanctions of the state — we can say that *political* integration has occurred. Focusing on political integration in this study will help us identify and emphasize the special problems experienced by the parties in South Africa that sought a conciliation of differences between the two white language groups, that is by the *parties of conciliation,* as we shall call

[4]Aristide R. Zolberg, "Patterns of National Integration," *Journal of Modern African Studies,* V, No. 4 (December 1967), 549.

them. Whereas an Afrikaner nationalist party might succeed
in becoming the governing party in the Union on the basis
of support given it by a single ethnic group, the position of
a party of conciliation was different. It could not hope to
secure power without support from *both* English-speaking
persons and Afrikaners. A party of conciliation therefore had
to bring about electoral cooperation among persons who
lacked strong mutual ties and whose capacity for political
cooperation was low. The task confronting an Afrikaner
nationalist party was easier, for those whose support it sought
were *already* united by a feeling of Afrikaner group identity
and self-awareness, and their capacity for collective political
action was accordingly high.

In fact, the problems facing the leaders of parties of
conciliation were much like those that confront leaders of
unification movements in international affairs. In a recent
work, Karl Deutsch has observed that in the early stages
of international unification movements political leadership
is commonly provided "not by a single social class but by
a cross-class coalition," and "major *political compromises* will
be needed to hold together these . . . coalitions whose members
are apt to be quite diverse in background, interests, and
outlook."[5] In South Africa, parties of conciliation, were
dependent on their leaders' capacities to compromise diver-
gent interests until such time as the political integration of
the two white language groups could be sufficiently advanced
to eliminate the need for such compromise.

But where the backgrounds, interests, and outlooks of the
associating groups are diverse, the discovery of "viable patterns of mutual political accommodation" takes time,
Deutsch writes, and the compromises involved are of a special
kind; they must not frustrate the parties by giving each much
less than it wants. On the contrary, the leaders must "discover
a way to exchange favors and to dovetail genuine and substantial concessions to one another's vital interests."[6] Mary
Parker Follett has called this method for dealing with conflict

[5]Karl W. Deutsch, *The Analysis of International Relations* (Eng-
lewood Cliffs, N.J.: Prentice-Hall, 1968), p. 199.
[6]*Ibid.*

"integration" in order to distinguish its special character from "domination," the victory of one side over the other, and "compromise," in which "each side gives up a little in order to have peace." Miss Follett identifies "integration" as a solution to conflict in which all desires find a place and no party is required to sacrifice anything. It "involves invention," she writes, "and the clever thing is to recognize this, and not to let one's thinking stay within the boundaries of two alternatives which are mutually exclusive."[7]

Substantively, it is my major conclusion herein that the failure of parties of conciliation in South Africa to attract lasting support from the Afrikaner electorate should be attributed to the inability of the leadership of these parties to invent "integrative" solutions (in Miss Follett's sense) for value conflicts between Afrikaners and English South Africans. In particular, I will argue that the successful insistence of Jan C. Smuts in September 1939 that the Union government declare war on Germany appeared to contradict the principle of "South Africa first" on which Afrikaners and English South Africans had come together in 1934, and that this decision released Afrikaners by the tens of thousands from adherence to the United Party that until that moment had been the embodiment of the policy of "conciliation." Even if these desertions were not so numerous as to result in the necessary defeat of the United Party at the next general election, as would seem to be the case, they did at least eliminate the electoral margin of safety for the government and thereby virtually ensured that Prime Minister Smuts would be beaten whenever the political tide should next turn against him. This view of the importance of the 1939 war vote for South African politics, and specifically its contribution to the defeat of Smuts in 1948, has largely been missed because it did not result in an immediate change of government, and four years later Smuts and the truncated United Party were returned to power at the general election of 1943. I will argue that the 1943 election results exaggerated the

[7]Henry C. Metcalf and L. Urwick (eds.), *Dynamic Administration: The Collected Papers of Mary Parker Follett* (New York and London: Harper and Bros., 1942), p. 31.

true level of partisan attachments to the United Party because of temporary and special political conditions. From this perspective, the victory of the Nationalists over Smuts in 1948 in terms of electoral realignment is less dramatic, and owes less to the eleventh-hour appeal of the doctrine of race "apartheid" than most students have customarily supposed.

1.

The Power of
Afrikaner Unity

ON June 17, 1929, South Africa's substantially white
and still wholly male electorate went to the polls in the
Union's sixth general election.[1] The results confirmed in power
the National Party-Labour Party coalition government that
had ruled since 1924, but changed the parliamentary balance
that had existed between the two coalition partners. The
National Party increased its number of MP's and for the
first time held an absolute majority (of eight) of the 148 seats
in the House of Assembly, but the Labour Party suffered
a loss of ten seats.[2] Prime Minister James B. M. Hertzog,
the leader of the National Party, agreed to continue the

[1] In 1929 there were 452,473 registered parliamentary voters, 41,744
of whom were nonwhites. All but 346 of the nonwhite voters were
in the Cape Province, and the remainder were in Natal. In 1930
white adult females were enfranchised, but not nonwhite females.
In 1936 Africans in the Cape Province were removed from the
general voters' roll, and thereafter until African representation in
Parliament was abolished altogether in 1960, they elected separately
three whites to represent their interests in the House of Assembly.
Similarly, Coloured voters were removed from the general voters'
roll in 1955 and thereafter allowed to elect four whites to the House
of Assembly until 1970 when their representation was ended. Asians
lost the general franchise in 1946 and all parliamentary representation in 1949.

[2] The House of Assembly is the lower house of the South African
Parliament, and the government-of-the-day is responsible to this
chamber. The upper house is the Senate. MP's are elected from
single-member constituencies. Senators are either nominated to the
Senate by the government or elected indirectly from each province
by electoral colleges consisting of provincial councilors and MP's
from that province. Between 1936 and 1960 there were in addition

7

coalition and two Labourites were taken into the new cabinet, but the Hertzog government was no longer dependent on Labour's support.

1929 Election Results

National Party	70
South African Party	61
Labour	8
Independents	1

There can be no doubt that the National Party achieved power in 1929 on the basis of the support given it by the Afrikaans-speaking electorate. The traditions of the party, the nature of its program, its literature in Afrikaans, and its largely rural base make it clear that few English South Africans voted for the National Party in 1929, and probably no non-whites did so. Yet for their part, Afrikaners appear to have been nearly unanimous in their support for the party. If we assume that all who voted for the National Party were Afrikaners, and include estimates of probable votes for un-contested constituencies, it seems likely that just over four-fifths of the Afrikaner portion of the electorate supported the National Party in 1929.

Who were these Afrikaners on whose support the 1929 government depended? Their origins lie in the fusion of immigrant communities of Dutch, French, and German extraction during the eighteenth century along the frontier of what is now the Cape Province. By 1800 these groups had been welded into a new and separate people, or *volk,* possessing distinctive characteristics. Among these were a unique language, a stern morality rooted in Calvinism, strong family ties, a pattern of life based on simple, rural values, and a sense of history that emphasized the wrongs suffered by the Afrikaners in the past, especially at the hands of Great Britain. In addition, in the words of F. A. van Jaarsveld, the Afrikaner exhibited ingrained personal traits of "independ-

---

four senators indirectly elected by Africans to represent African interests in the Senate. By law, all MP's and senators must be white men or women.

ence, dexterity, stubborness, resoluteness against force, and love of freedom and of the veld with its wide open spaces."[3] All of these continued to be characteristics of Afrikaners throughout the nineteenth century, and by 1910 Afrikaners had, in addition, developed a group feeling — national self-consciousness, or nationalism. This spirit had been born of the pressures of British imperial policy upon the two Boer republics after 1871. The South African War, especially, "taught the Afrikaners that they were a people."[4] This sense of Afrikaner nationhood was of the greatest importance at the time of Union, because as the first Union census was to show in 1911, Afrikaners had already come to constitute approximately 54 per cent of the white inhabitants of the country, upon whom the new constitution placed nearly exclusive responsibility for determining the Union's political future.[5] Were Afrikaners to act together, it was clear that they would be able to dominate in politics. The political unity of the Afrikaner Volk was thus from the outset the decisive factor in the public affairs of South Africa.

In fact, Afrikaners *entered* the Union politically united, but this unity was seemingly in support of "conciliation" rather than of Afrikaner nationalism. During the colonial period after the South African War, political parties were organized by the defeated Boers in both of the former republics. In 1905 in the Transvaal, Louis Botha, the former Commandant-General of the Boer forces, founded Het Volk (The People) in order to represent and protect Afrikaner interests. But Botha had no wish that his party should represent Afrikaner interests only, or that cooperation with the "well-disposed English," in D. W. Kruger's words, should be precluded.[6] Like the older South African Party in the Cape

[3]F. A. van Jaarveld, *The Awakening of Afrikaner Nationalism 1868-1881*, trans. F. R. Metrowich (Cape Town: Human & Rousseau, 1961), p. 11.
[4]Eric A. Walker, *A History of Southern Africa* (London: Longmans, Green, 1962), p. 513.
[5]Leonard M. Thompson, *The Unification of South Africa, 1902-1910* (Oxford, Clarendon Press, 1960), p. 15n.
[6]D. W. Kruger (ed.), *South African Parties and Policies 1910-1960: A Select Source Book* (Cape Town: Human & Rousseau, 1960), p. viii.

Colony, Het Volk, although jealous for the rights of Afrikaners, sought realization of a broad South African nationalism that might be shared by both Afrikaners and English-
speaking colonists. In the Orange River Colony, the Orangia
Unie, founded a year after Het Volk, had narrower aims. It
was concerned with Afrikaner interests solely, and "the
Afrikaner cultural motive was strongly stressed."[7] At the time
of acceptance of the draft constitution in 1909, it seemed
likely that the Orangia Unie would provide the base for the
development of a country-wide political body committed to
exclusive Afrikaner aims, but this did not occur, at least not
immediately. General Hertzog, the leader of the Orangia Unie
and widely regarded as the foremost Afrikaner nationalist
of the day, consented to join the first Union cabinet under
Prime Minister Botha, and the Orangia Unie worked with
Het Volk and the South African Party in support of the new
government in the first general election of 1910. After this
election the three colonial parties merged to form the new
South African National Party. The 1910 election was a
considerable personal triumph for Botha and a victory for
"conciliation," as the new Prime Minister termed his policy.
The government obtained the nearly unanimous support of
Afrikaners and had bridged as well the gap between them
and the English-speaking community. With the support of
four Labour MP's, Botha had a majority of 21 in the first
House of Assembly.

1910 Election Results

South African National Party	66
Unionists	38
Labour	4
Independents	13

For awhile it appeared that "conciliation" might capture
the imagination of most Afrikaners. Even Hertzog, the most
nasionale-gesinde (national-minded) of cabinet ministers,
seemed ready to respond to the optimism with which all

[7]*Ibid.*

sections of the white population greeted Union. At a Pretoria congress of the South African National Party in 1912, Hertzog seconded a motion to delete "national" from the name of the body because it referred too much to the Afrikaner group. "Our wish", he said, "is to form a party which will embrace all white people in South Africa."[8] But this unity of purpose did not last. Soon a schism developed between Botha and Hertzog, and in the end it split the new political unity of Afrikaners and led to the founding in 1914 of the National Party to articulate and defend purely Afrikaner national interests. At first the National Party enjoyed significant support only in the Orange Free State. Only six of that province's seventeen MP's joined the new party, but guided by such pre-Union leaders as General Christiaan R. de Wet and former President M. T. Steyn, as well as Hertzog, most of the Afrikaner electorate in the Free State soon swung behind the Nationalists. In the Cape and the Transvaal, the leaders of the National Party were comparatively little-known men, and there were few followers; in Natal the party was nonexistent. Yet at the general election of 1915, the Nationalists captured 28 percent of the vote (including estimates for uncontested seats) and 27 of 130 seats in the House of Assembly, and only nine years later Hertzog became the country's third prime minister. The Hertzog government elected in 1924 was a coalition, dependent for its existence on the votes of 18 Labour MP's, but this dependence scarcely detracted from the political triumph that had been achieved by the Nationalists in just over a decade: 111,000 electors, or 35 percent of all voters, supported the National Party in 1924; this number was only 37,000 less than the number of voters who supported the South African Party, although it had absorbed the sizable Unionist Party in 1920. With more seats than any other party in the House of Assembly, the Nationalists in 1924 were supreme in most of the country districts of both the Transvaal and the Cape, and they

[8]L. E. Neame, *General Hertzog: Prime Minister of the Union of South Africa Since 1924* (London: Hurst & Blackett, [193?]), p. 112.

controlled all but one of the Free State constituencies. Five years later at the general election of 1929, the Nationalist vote increased by a further 30,000, to 40 percent of all votes cast, as against an increase of only 11,000 for the South African Party. Labour's total vote meanwhile dropped by 11,000, down to 34,000. Thus at the beginning of 1914 nearly all Afrikaners were at least nominally supporters of the South African Party's policy of "conciliation," but fifteen years later four of five Afrikaners appeared to support Afrikaner nationalism. In the words of Eric A. Walker, by 1929 "party divisions had drifted perilously near the so-called racial line," that is, the line separating Afrikaners from men of British stock.[9]

Stimulants of Afrikaner Nationalism

As all recent voting studies have shown, people support political parties for a broad variety of reasons. Certainly many factors contributed to the steady rise of the National Party in South Africa between its founding in 1914 and the 1929 election. Yet all the most obvious factors appear to have been associated with a growing group anxiety on the part of Afrikaners during this period, coupled with an acceptance of the National Party as the political remedy. This group anxiety had two faces. On the one hand, it arose in part out of the increasing sense of Afrikaners at this time that they, as a group, were relatively deprived compared with the white English-speaking community in South Africa. It has often been observed that a sense of relative deprivation has been an inspiration of most nationalisms. As early as 1935, for example, Harold Lasswell noted that "the demand to be emancipated from an inferior status is one component of those national, racial, and labor movements which have figured so prominently in recent years."[10] Racial fears of nonwhite advance provided the other aspect of this group anxiety, although in practice both themes were often intertwined, as we shall see below. In matters of race, obviously, the reference group was not the Afrikaans-speaking community per se but

[9]Walker, *A History of Southern Africa,* p. 625.
[10]Harold D. Lasswell, *World Politics and Personal Insecurity* (New York: Whittlesey House, 1935), p. 94.

whites generally; but as van Jaarsveld has suggested, race consciousness has been an especially notable feature of the Afrikaner's social motive, or modal personality.[11] Moreover, because of their often greater proximity to nonwhites in the economic hierarchy, Afrikaans-speaking workers in particular appeared to have most to lose from a lowering of the color bars. It would seem that feelings of group anxiety may be experienced on any or all of Max Weber's three dimensions of social inequality: class, status, and power,[12] and indeed in the case of the growth of Afrikaner nationalism up to 1929, questions arising out of each of these dimensions were clearly involved.

Class Issues

Economic considerations certainly played an important role. An economic slump in South Africa followed the immediate post-World War I boom, and with this downturn came shortages in both housing and jobs. Simultaneously, the country suffered its worst drought in fifty years, and thousands of impoverished and unskilled "poor whites" were forced out of the rural areas and into the cities. Unprepared psychologically because of race pride to do the manual work which was the only urban employment for which they were really equipped, these persons looked without success to the central government for their economic salvation. Moreover, the government's military suppression of the Johannesburg miners' strike in 1922 resulted in wholesale defections of white workers from the ruling South African Party, and after that these persons enthusiastically supported the pact that was soon formed between Labour and the Nationalists.[13] The impact

[11]On the concept of "social motive," see Philip E. Jacob and Henry Teune, "The Integrative Process: Guidelines for Analysis of the Bases of Political Community," in Philip E. Jacob and James V. Toscano (eds.), *The Integration of Political Communities* (Philadelphia and New York: J. B. Lippincott Co., 1964), pp. 32-35.

[12]See H. H. Gerth and C. Wright Mills (eds.), *From Max Weber* (New York: Oxford University Press, 1958), especially Chapter VII. For a contemporary discussion of these dimensions, see W. G. Runciman, *Relative Deprivation and Social Justice* (London: Routledge & Kegan Paul, 1966), Chapter 3.

[13]E. S. Sachs, *The Choice Before South Africa* (London: Turnstile Press, 1952), p. 153.

of these events was especially great among Afrikaners, who shortly came to believe that they "had first to gain, and then to maintain, political power or be submerged as an economic group."[14]

But if economic conditions cost the government Afrikaans-speaking support before 1924, after that date the state of the economy had the opposite result. Hertzog had hardly taken office when South Africa's material prospects suddenly brightened. Good rains fell again on the parched earth, and the worldwide depression gave way to a time of prosperity. South Africa entered upon an unprecedented economic boom. Moreover, the Labour and National Parties worked together more easily in power than many had thought possible, and the rapid increase in the number of Afrikaners within the urban labor force, especially in the gold mines, provided a growing common interest and drew the two parties together. The Pact government soon moved to protect white workers — and in practice these were mostly Afrikaners — from the competition of nonwhites. Government departments were instructed to employ whites instead of nonwhites whenever possible — the so-called "civilized labour policy." In 1926 passage of the controversial Colour Bar Bill extended to other fields the white monopoly of skilled and semiskilled positions that had existed in the mining industry since 1911.

Status Issues

Cultural issues, especially concerning language, were at the root of the status anxiety of Afrikaners, which was most of all a sense of relative status deprivation vis-à-vis English-speaking South Africa. Such feelings were an inevitable outgrowth of the British victory in the South African War, but they were aggravated by Lord Milner's deliberate efforts to give an emphatically British bias to the new postwar system of public education in South Africa. Indeed, by increasing the determination of the Boers that the Dutch language and Dutch traditions should have a respected place in state affairs, Milner's policy provided dramatic confirmation of David Easton's point that attempts at forced assimilation may be

[14]Stanley Trapido, "Political Institutions and Afrikaner Social Structure in the Republic of South Africa," *American Political Science Review*, LVII, No. 1 (March 1963), 76.

the *least* effective way of achieving an integrated political system.[15] Soon after Union, in 1913, a strong cultural movement centering on the use of the Afrikaans language reappeared within the Afrikaans-speaking population. As would be the case in many of the new independent black states to the north half a century later, the enlargement of the political sphere had had the effect of politicizing primary ties.[16] Increasingly, Afrikaners came to feel strongly about their language and their culture and to feel alien in the South African Party, which was suspected of being dominated by "influences rooted in the British way of living."[17] Botha tried to allay this feeling, but the Nationalists were more successful in identifying with the cultural sentiments of Afrikaners, and to a great extent the National Party was accepted as the "political counterpart of the cultural movement."[18] Thus while in its formal organization and activities the National Party resembled other political parties of the time, it came to be closely allied for purposes of recruitment and the dissemination of its propaganda with other "national-minded" bodies such as the Dutch Reformed Churches and various Afrikaner cultural organizations. This gained for the National Party valuable resources for the political struggle that none of its opponents could equal in kind. Botha's death in 1919 released many of his personal supporters from their allegiance to the South African Party, and his succession by Smuts lost the government more support, for Smuts' rise in the councils of the British Empire had only confirmed the suspicions of many Afrikaners that he had lost interest in the Volk. The acceptability of the South African Party to Afrikaners was further decreased in 1920 by its fusion with the openly pro-British Unionist Party, even though Smuts agreed to this fusion only after an attempt at reunion with the Nationalists had failed.

[15]David Easton, *A Systems Analysis of Political Life* (New York: John Wiley & Sons, 1967), p. 250.
[16]Aristide R. Zolberg, *Creating Political Order* (Chicago: Rand McNally, 1966), p. 22.
[17]D. W. Kruger, *The Age of the Generals* (Johannesburg: Dagbreek Book Store, 1966), p. 72.
[18]*Ibid.*, p. 111.

The urbanization of Afrikaans-speaking "poor whites" in the 1920's, previously referred to, created not only class anxieties but feelings of relative *status* deprivation as well. David Welsh reminds us that "it is common for townspeople to have an unfavorable image of rural people, regarding them as slow-witted, ill-educated, gauche, and simple." But because in South Africa the urban-rural cleavage among whites largely coincided with the Afrikaans-English ethnic cleavage, the social distance between the older and newer urban residents was particularly great. "The reception that many Afrikaner immigrants from the rural areas received in the towns was not a friendly one," Welsh writes, and many found themselves at a decided disadvantage because the language of commerce and industry was English.[19] Further, as has been indicated, the economic imperative for these urban migrants to perform menial laboring tasks for a low wage conflicted with a sense of their own dignity conferred on them by race. For Afrikaners born on the land, quoting C. W. de Kiewiet, "to be hirelings was bad enough. To have to do work commonly done by natives was offensive."[20] It is sometimes supposed that urbanization assists the development of tolerant social attitudes in individuals, for the hetrogeneity of urban life would seem to encourage contact with persons of diverse backgrounds, and some aspects of the cultures of other groups are likely to be assimilated. In 1960, for example, Rupert Emerson speculated that "the most hopeful prospect is that the Afrikaner community may gradually recognize the need for [race] policies more in keeping with the modern world as more of its members are drawn into urban industrial and commercial life."[21] The validity of this projection in the case of urban Afrikaners has been questioned by H. Lever and O. J. M. Wagner, who report the results of a recent survey that shows

[19]David Welsh, "Urbanisation and the Solidarity of Afrikaner Nationalism," *Journal of Modern African Studies,* VII, No. 2 (July 1969), 265-266.
[20]C. W. de Kiewiet, *A History of South Africa: Social and Economic* (London: Oxford University Press, 1957), p. 216.
[21]Rupert Emerson, *From Empire to Nation: The Rise to Self-Assertion of Asian and African Peoples* (Cambridge: Harvard University Press, 1960), p. 340.

no relationship between the extent of urbanization and either unfavorable attitudes toward Africans or belief in the policy of "apartheid."[22] In any case, the projection is a long-term one. In the short run, it seems clear that newly urban Afrikaners felt embattled by English-speaking whites, with their powerful urban culture, as well as by nonwhites, with whom they were now often in direct economic competition. The result helped bring Hertzog to power in 1924, and, indeed, through the associated feelings of both class and status anxiety it engendered among Afrikaner "poor whites," urbanization fed the fires of Afrikaner nationalism throughout at least the first four decades of Union.

In power after 1924 as before, Hertzog and his fellow Nationalists assiduously catered to the cultural sentiments of Afrikaners, as Smuts had often unwittingly or necessarily ignored them. In 1925 Afrikaans was recognized as an official language of the Union, a momentous decision politically, and an official grant was made for the compiling of an Afrikaans dictionary.[23] And for the first time bilingualism was enforced in the civil service, proficiency in both languages becoming a prerequisite for promotion. Also in 1925 His Majesty was asked to refrain henceforth from conferring further honorific titles on persons living in South Africa or South-West Africa.

Power Issues

Feelings of power anxiety among Afrikaners exhibited themselves in the continuing currency of the issue of the Union's political independence, although this issue can be linked to Afrikaner feelings of relative status deprivation as well. The issue of political independence was, of course, an important focus of Afrikaner group sentiment long before 1910. In the first half of the nineteenth century, the Voortrekkers sought political independence from the British Em-

[22]H. Lever and O. J. M. Wagner, "Urbanization and the Afrikaner," *Race*, XI, No. 2 (October 1969), 186.
[23]The South Africa Act of 1909 recognized both English and Dutch as official languages of the Union. Act No. 8 of 1925 amended the South Africa Act to broaden the meaning of "Dutch" to include Afrikaans.

pire in order to guarantee the local dominance of and, indeed, the survival of their distinctive social and cultural values, while at the end of the same century the foremost object of the governments of the two Boer republics was the maintenance of their sovereignty. In Afrikaans, the South African War is termed "The Second War for Independence," the first being the Transvaal "rebellion" against the British in 1881. Except for the unsuccessful insurrection in 1914 of several thousand Afrikaners in the Transvaal and the Free State — they saw in Britain's military preoccupations in Europe a chance to regain the lost sovereignty of these provinces — after 1910 Afrikaner nationalists sought the independence of the Union as a whole. Independence now became a test of the domestic cultural and political equality of the two white groups, and a matter of international political rectitude as well.

Believing that his difference with Prime Minister Botha was his insistence that South Africa's interests be considered ahead of those of the Empire, Hertzog was ejected from the first Union Cabinet in 1912. For his part, Botha was more concerned with Hertzog's public repudiation of the doctrine of "conciliation." In fact, the two issues were joined in Hertzog's mind, although he seldom expressed his ideas clearly. By 1912 Hertzog had come to believe that most English South Africans were wedded to the imperial ideal, and that because of the strength of British influences in South Africa, Botha's policy of "conciliation" was likely to compromise South African independence. Out of the cabinet, Hertzog traveled from village to village in the Free State in 1913 spreading "the old gospel of Colonial Nationalism and self-government applied very narrowly to South African conditions and to Dutch ideals in particular," and these speeches met with a considerable response.[24] Everywhere Hertzog spoke, Afrikaner "vigilance committees" sprang into being. According to F. S. Crafford, Hertzog at this time weaned

[24]Neame, *General Hertzog,* p. 150.

thousands of Afrikaners away from the South African Party.[25].

Botha's commitment of the Union in 1914 to what was to become a long, tedious, and in some measure unpopular war in Europe increased Afrikaner agitation on the issue of national independence, and Afrikaner nationalist sentiment was scarcely lessened by Botha's necessary military suppression of the 1914 rebellion. But the issue of independence did not pass at the war's end. In 1919 the Nationalists dispatched a delegation to the Peace Conference at Versailles to demand independence for the Union, or if that were not possible, restoration of the former republics, and although the delegation failed to realize either goal, it scored a propaganda triumph at home. The idea of restoring the two Boer republics is significant, for this was the last time that responsible Afrikaner leaders proposed to relieve feelings of relative power and status deprivation among Afrikaners vis-à-vis English South Africa through a political partition of the Union. (This idea, of course, made no reference to nonwhites. Four decades later, however, it would be possible to interpret the government's "Bantustan" program as an effort to prevent *future* power and status deprivation of whites vis-à-vis nonwhites by a racial partition of the country.) An obvious reason for dropping this idea was the awareness that since insurrection and persuasion had already failed, partition would require the winning of political power, and if this could be done a partition would no longer be necessary to secure Afrikaner interests. But there may have been another reason as well. Between 1904 and 1911, the proportion of all whites living in the Transvaal rose from 18.6 percent to 32.9 percent, and there can be little doubt that non-Afrikaners accounted for much of this increase. Indeed, by the time of the 1911 census, only 48.5 percent of all whites in the Transvaal were affiliated with the Dutch Reformed Churches; Leonard Thompson suggests this statistic is probably a good approximation of

[25]F. S. Crafford, *Jan Smuts: A Biography* (Cape Town: Howard B. Timmins, 1945), p. 99.

the Afrikaner proportion in the white population.[26] In short, shifts within the white population in the decades following the South African War — which continued demographic changes that began with the discovery of gold on the Witwatersrand in the 1880s — challenged the idea underlying the partition approach, that the Transvaal (in addition to the Orange Free State) was an Afrikaner "homeland." I am suggesting that Afrikaner nationalist strategy was necessarily influenced not only by the ethnic composition of the white population but also by its spatial distribution. In any event, in 1921 the National Party pledged to work for the realization of "sovereign independence for South Africa [as a whole] separated from the United Kingdom and/or British Empire,"[27] although three years later, a condition of the National Party-Labour Party alliance, extracted by the Labour Party, was that: "In the next Parliament . . . elected, should a Nationalist Government come into power, no Nationalist member of Parliament will use his vote to upset the existing Consitutional arrangement of South Africa to the British Crown."[28]

In 1926 as premier, Hertzog attended an imperial conference that agreed — largely in response to his urgings — to the statement (the so-called Balfour Declaration) that Great Britain and the Dominions "are autonomous communities within the British Empire, equal in status, in no way subordinate the one to the other in any aspect of their internal or external affairs."[29] After his return to South Africa, Hertzog maintained that "the old British Empire which existed in the past . . . exists no longer" and that henceforth South Africa should be regarded as completely sovereign and independent.[30] Thereafter, the government sponsored legislation providing for a Union nationality, supplementing the existing British citizenship of South Africans, and a South African national flag was designed and its flying authorized

[26]Thompson, *The Unification of South Africa*, p. 15n.
[27]Neame, *General Hertzog*, p. 223.
[28]Kruger (ed.), *South African Parties and Policies*, p. 75.
[29]*Ibid.*, p. 145.
[30]Neame, *General Hertzog*, p. 253.

alongside the Union Jack, symbolizing respectively South Africa's national sovereignty and membership in the British Commonwealth. These constitutional accomplishments of the Hertzog government gratified many Afrikaners who were anxious that South Africa be relieved of all vestiges of subservience to Great Britain, but not all agreed with Hertzog, who suggested in 1927 that the Balfour Declaration had settled the question of South Africa's constitutional freedom. Many Afrikaners remained ardent republicans, irrevocably suspicious of Britain and English-speaking persons and able to see nothing beneficial in the imperial connection. Hertzog asserted that he continued to view a republic as the ideal form of government and believed that 99 of 100 Nationalists were in favor of a republic, but he insisted that the National Party had never made republicanism a prerequisite for membership. Republicanism was not practical politics, Hertzog maintained.[31] This was a severe blow to a great number of Nationalists who in their hearts still held that true South African independence was only possible apart from the British Empire. After 1927, Afrikaner republicans began to lose faith in Hertzog, and while they continued to support him, they looked increasingly to Dr. Daniel F. Malan, head of the party in the Cape Province, as their leader. Moreover, because of his uncompromising stance during the bitter controversy over the flag question in 1926, Malan similarly came to be regarded by his opponents *outside* the National party as the leader of the extreme wing of Afrikaner nationalism.

Finally, there was the issue of race, which may be interpreted as also giving evidence of white, and particularly Afrikaner, power anxiety. At the beginning of 1929 Hertzog had proceeded with two parliamentary bills that would have brought changes in the nonwhite franchise and thus dealt with matters that were "entrenched" in the South Africa Act. Enactment of either bill therefore required the two-thirds support of both Houses of Parliament, sitting together. When the vote on the first bill, which would have removed Africans from the common voters' roll in the Cape Province, fell short of the necessary majority, Hertzog asked that the House of Assem-

[31]*Ibid.*

bly be dissolved and went to the country on the question of the Union's race policy. During the campaign the Nationalists singled out Smuts and directed most of their fire at him personally. The most telling blow was directed at Smuts' alleged willingness to share power with black Africans. In January 1929, in a speech at Ermelo in the Transvaal, Smuts had recommended South African cooperation with other British African territories, leading to an African federation of states. The speech was the basis of a Nationalist charge during the campaign that Smuts was a man "who puts himself forward as the apostle of a black Kafir State, of which South Africa is to form so subordinate a part that she will know her own name no more."[32] The Nationalists placed before the electorate the choice between their own rule and a white South Africa, on the one hand, and a Smuts ministry and a black state in which whites would have no chance, on the other. Although it distorted Smuts' true attitude on race policy, this tactic succeeded in playing on the racial prejudices and insecurities of Afrikaners, especially in the urban centers, where issues of both status and class also placed Afrikaner "poor whites" in direct opposition to the African proletariat.

[32]The 1929 National Party election manifesto, quoted by Neame, *General Hertzog*, p. 270.

2.

Fusion

KARL Deutsch maintains that the integrative process does *not* consist of a prescribed series of stages through which a community must pass as it comes into being.[1] Rather, Deutsch argues, integrated communities are assembled in all their essential aspects in the course of history, "somewhat as an automibile is put together;" and as in the assembly of a car, it matters little in what sequence each element is added so long as in the end all the important elements have found their place. Nevertheless, Deutsch states that as a *political* process, integration does have a *takeoff point* in time when it ceases being "a matter of a few prophets or scattered and powerless supporters, but turns into a larger and more coordinated movement with some significant power behind it." Integrative "takeoff" is that moment referred to in the Introduction when major political compromises result in a coalition of diverse political interests capable of providing effective leadership toward unification. Such a moment, Deutsch writes, usually requires that three conditions be present. First, "a new and attractive way of life" has to emerge, giving the groups concerned "some latent sense of unity of outlook and interests." Second, it is necessary that some external challenge appear, arousing this latent sense of unity and requiring a new and joint response. And third, a new generation of persons is needed on the political scene. Deutsch suggests this last event is likely to occur roughly every fifteen years.[2] In South Africa, such conditions were present in the

[1]Deutsch, *The Analysis of International Relations.*
[2]*Ibid.*, pp. 196-199.

early 1930s and contributed to a renewal of efforts at "conciliation" between Afrikaners and English South Africans. These
efforts resulted in 1934 in the political union of the South
African and National Parties. In retrospect, "Fusion," as this
union was known, can be seen to have constituted an integrative "takeoff." Fusion was possible in 1934, as it had not been
possible in 1920, because time, and the achievements of the
Pact government, had eroded the old divisions between Boers
and Britons and had caused an increasing number of Afrikaners to perceive the beginnings of a new South African
way of life among whites. Indeed, as Hertzog himself noted,
the movement within the National Party toward Fusion was
strongest in the Transvaal, that is, among comparative new-
comers to the party,[3] which would seem to confirm the
importance Deutsch ascribes to the arrival of a new political
generation. But the greatest impetus to Fusion was the
worldwide economic depression of the 1930s.

The impact of the depression on South Africa was serious,
especially in the rural areas, where difficulties were compounded by the worst drought in history. Between 1926 and
1931, the rural areas of the Cape Province and the Orange
Free State experienced an absolute decrease in their popula-
tions as thousands moved to the cities looking for work.[4] In
the cities, unemployment mounted, for industry could not
absorb the unskilled persons who suddenly thrust themselves
on the labor market. The Carnegie Commission calculated
that in the period 1929-1930, some 300,000 white South
Africans were "very poor," and many of these were thought
to be Afrikaners.[5] Had the National Party been in opposition,
this economic distress would certainly have been a stimulant
to Afrikaner nationalism. But the National Party was the
government, and in meeting the crisis, it appeared to falter.

[3]See Hertzog's remarks to the Free State Head Committee of the
National Party, September 7, 1933, quoted in *The Cape Times,*
September 8, 1933.
[4]J. F. S. Grosskopf, *Economic Report: Rural impoverishment and
rural exodus,* vol. I of *The Poor White Problem in South Africa:
The Report of the Carnegie Commission* (Stellenbosch: Pro Ecclesia-Drukkery, 1932), p. I-70.
[5]*Ibid.,* pp. vii and I-4.

The government failed to provide relief for the farmers, and many of its economy measures adversely affected Afrikaners in the towns. Meanwhile, new taxes appeared to bear disproportionately on the clerk and the artisan. *Round Table* reported that there were "many outward murmurings in the railway camps and on the farms."[6] Prime Minister Hertzog's insistence that the Union remain on the gold standard (in part to demonstrate the Union's independence from Great Britain, which abandoned the gold standard in 1931) was widely unpopular, and many felt that this decision was at the root of South Africa's troubles. Parliamentary by-elections in 1930 and 1932 demonstrated that the government was losing popular support to the South African Party, the only alternative. Concurrently, Hertzog's position in the House weakened. At one division in 1932 on a salary-reduction bill, the government's majority was only five. Three years earlier, Hertzog had been able to count on a majority of 25 for most purposes.

On February 10, 1933, Hertzog issued a public statement that was virtually an offer to form a coalition government including Smuts and the South African Party.[7] Smuts responded favorably, and five days later private negotiations were begun. Hertzog and Smuts soon came to an agreement: a coalition government would be formed. The cabinet would be enlarged to twelve members, and both the National Party and the South African party would hold six portfolios. Hertzog would continue as prime minister, while Smuts would become depty prime minister. The government would not proceed with Hertzog's bills affecting the nonwhite franchise, but the "Native question would be solved in such a way as to safeguard White civilization." Finally, after several other points, it was agreed that Parliament would be dissolved and an early election called to test the popular support of the new ministry.[8] These terms were subsequently ratified by the two parties, although in the case of the National Party the

[6]*Round Table,* No. 83 (June, 1931), p. 674.
[7]*Round Table,* No. 91 (June, 1933), p. 689.
[8]For more details of the coalition agreement, see Kruger, *Age of the Generals,* p. 160, or Oswald Pirow, *James Barry Munnik Hertzog* (Cape Town: Howard Timmins, [1957]), p. 157.

support of Dr. Malan and the Cape branch was given with obvious reluctance. The new ministry was sworn in on March 31. In April the House of Assembly was dissolved and elections called for May 17. The ensuing campaign was notable for the absence of the usual election-time bitterness, for under the coalition agreement each of the two parties kept those seats in the new Parliament that it had held before, subject, of course, to such election losses as occurred. Indeed, 78 candidates, all supporters of the coalition, were returned unopposed. The results of the election gave the coalition the support of 136 of the 150 MP's in the new House.

As had been the case nine years earlier, formation of a new government in 1933 marked the beginning of better times for South Africa.[9] In the preceding December, the Union had been forced to leave the gold standard, and now money flowed back into the country and was once again plentiful. Rains ended the long drought. Revenues mounted, allowing the government to decrease taxation and extend financial assistance to the agricultural community, and additional schemes were undertaken for the rehabilitation of farmers. Rates for workmen's compensation and medical payments for lung disease among miners were increased, while help was offered to the municipalities for slum clearance. A ten-year plan for development of the railways was inaugurated. Concurrent with these developments, a spontaneous public movement for the permanent union, or fusion, of the two coalition parties developed. At the local level there was a growing tendency for branches of the two parties to amalgamate, and this trend was especially strong in the rural areas of the Orange Free State and the Transvaal.[10] The fusion movement was not without its opponents in both wings of the coalition, however. In the National Party opposition was widespread in the Cape Province, and it existed to a lesser degree in the Free State. On October 13, 1933, the Federal Council of the National Party, its national governing body, authorized Hertzog to meet with Smuts for the purpose of drawing up a proposed set of principles for a new united party. This decision accorded

[9]Walker, *A History of Southern Africa,* p. 637.
[10]Kruger, *Age of the Generals,* p. 163.

with pro-fusion resolutions that had been adopted by the party in the Transvaal, Natal, and the Orange Free State. But the National Party in the Cape refused to endorse fusion, and at the meeting of the Federal Council, Malan indicated the readiness of the Cape branch of the party to stand apart and maintain its own identity should fusion occur.

In January 1934, Malan indicated a willingness to meet with Hertzog to try to reconcile differences between the Cape National Party and the Prime Minister, and shortly thereafter the two leaders came together at Groote Schuur, the official residence of South African premiers outside Cape Town. Whether this meeting and several related conversations and letters that followed it were serious efforts to negotiate a settlement, or only attempts on the part of one or both camps to compile a public record that would bolster a course of action already decided upon, these discussions revealed the primacy of the issue of national independence in the final split in the National Party that was to occur in June and, accordingly, merit the detailed treatment below. First, however, we shall introduce the concept of a "consummatory" value to help identify the reason for the special importance of the issue of national independence, and why its resolution was so difficult.

In his brilliant if sometimes confusing work, *The Politics of Modernization,* David Apter distinguishes between two types of social values. A "value," in Apter's sense, following general social science usage, is any object or act that is needed or desired. If a desired object or act is deemed to have importance, or relevance, because it is seen to lie in close relationship to an ultimate, or cosmological, or sacred end of society, such an object or act, according to Apter, is a *consummatory* value. If, however, the meaning of a desired object or act is independent of ultimate or sacred ends and instead is related to ends that are fragmentary, immediate, and verifiable, Apter calls it an *instrumental* value. An important difference is that methodologically, consummatory values are nonrational in that their consequences cannot be examined empirically, and they are, moreover, highly resistant to negotiation, compromise, and, indeed, change. In contrast, instrumental values have consequences that can be examined, and in principle they are subject to negotiation and compromise through rational bargaining. "Most economic objectives," Apter writes, "are of this nature."[11]

In South Africa, the national independence of the Union was a consummatory value for both Afrikaner nationalists and Empire loyalists, although in opposite ways. (Indeed, because the Afrikaner nationalist was a nationalist, he tended to view *all* points of difference between Afrikaners and non-Afrikaners as aspects of the seamless fabric of Afrikaner nationhood. This naturally compounded the problems of inter-group accommodation: cleavages based on class or region, for example, being largely instrumental in nature, might have been more easily reconciled.) For the Afrikaner nationalist, independence of the Union not only signified release from the humiliation of defeat in the South African War, it was also perceived as a prerequisite for realization of the full *moral* potentialities of the Afrikaner nation, if not of the South African nation. Malan typified this attitude and conveyed the distinctively consummatory nature of the issue when as Minister of the Interior in 1926 he defended in Parliament the government's South African Nationality and Flag Bill as follows:

> This Bill has got nothing to do, at least it has got nothing directly to do, with the material welfare of the country. It has no direct connection with what is generally called "bread-and-butter politics," important and necessary as "bread-and-butter politics" may be in its place. On the other hand, it has to do with the nation itself. It has to do with the very existence of the nation as a separate entity. It has to do with the unity of our national life and sentiment. It has to do with our national status and the recognition of our national status by other nations of the world. It has to do with what is more than material possessions, with what is, after all, even more than our fatherland; it has to do with the soul of the nation.[12]

[11]David E. Apter, *The Politics of Modernization* (Chicago and London: University of Chicago Press, 1965), pp. 83-85, 250.
[12]Kruger (ed.), *South African Parties and Policies,* p. 122.

Of course, most nationalisms give emphasis to the matter of national independence, but the Afrikaner's distinctive history has set the value of independence for the Afrikaner nationalist especially high, while the theological justification that Calvinism provides for the existence and authority of the State has linked the issue to his most profound understanding of the nature of human existence.

The Empire loyalist, too, saw political independence for the Union affecting the "soul" of South Africa, but in an adverse manner. For him, the British "connexion" was a valued tradition and heritage, and even after the 1926 Balfour Declaration, and the Statute of Westminster of 1931 which enacted its meaning into British law, he continued to regard the Crown as indivisible: that is, in time of war the Commonwealth was inescapably united. Far from demeaning South Africa, the Empire loyalist believed that the Commonwealth offered the Union and its people a continuity with an honored past, lifting them out of parochial sentiments to membership in a magnificent worldwide civilization. To break its connection with Britain, he thought, could only impoverish South Africa, for what the Afrikaner nationalist viewed as the dignity and honor of equal standing with the nations of the world, the Empire loyalist regarded as the provincialism and powerlessness of isolation, and the shallowness of immaturity. For him, commonwealth was superior to nationhood as a basis of social organization because it was more ennobling.

Putting the matter this way emphasizes not only the consummatory quality of the issue of national independence for many white South Africans, but also the incompatibility of the two positions described. Naturally, there were some whites who were neither Afrikaner nationalists nor Empire loyalists on this issue and for whom the matter of national independence may not have involved ultimate ends. But it would seem that there were comparatively few such persons. At the time of Union, and periodically thereafter, other differences between Boers and Britons were frequently reconciled by accepting a considerable cultural dualism in the public life of South Africa. In 1934, the Union had two official languages, two capital cities (three, if the judicial capital at

Bloemfontein is included), and two national flags. By 1938, South Africa would in addition have de facto two national anthems, "God Save the Queen" and "Die Stem." These arrangements were less than fully satisfying for many whites; equal treatment failed to accord to either anthem the singular place of honor some would have preferred. Nevertheless, such a pattern of dualism in South African national life provided a workable, if occasionally cumbersome, modus operandi. On the question of national independence, however, and specifically on the question of the divisibility of the Crown, such an "integrative" solution was not available. South Africa might be wholly independent, or it might be obliged — morally, if not legally — to come to the defense of the Commonwealth in wartime, but it could not conceivably be both independent and committed in advance to defending imperial interests. Nor could the matter be dealt with through compromise because of the consummatory, or non-negotiable, nature of the conflicting positions. Short of the domination of one view over the other, the issue of national independence in South Africa in the 1930s was ultimately insoluble; it could only be obscured or ignored. Indeed, it was in large measure the fear that the issue *was* being ignored by Hertzog at the time of Fusion that motivated the Cape dissidents within the National Party.

We can now return to the negotiations between Hertzog and Malan that took place on February 4 and 6, 1934. Malan urged the Prime Minister to agree to three points: the right of members of the proposed new party to propagandize for a republic; the need to abolish the right of appeal to the Privy Council; and the desirability of appointing an Afrikaner as the next Governor-General. Hertzog responded that he had no objection to a clause being inserted in the constitution of the new party that should make it permissible for a member to propagandize for any form of government he chose.[13] He agreed further that he would abolish the right to appeal to the Privy Council once pending appeals had been disposed of, and he pledged to advise the King to appoint a South African as the next Governor-General if he were still prime

[13]C. M. van den Heever, *General J. B. M. Hertzog* (Johannesburg: A. P. B. Bookstore, 1946), p. 254.

minister at the time. His demands substantially met, Malan indicated that the Cape congress of the National Party was now ready to accept Fusion in principle,[14] but a few days later, F. C. Erasmus wrote to the Prime Minister on behalf of the Cape head committee requesting additional assurances. Between February 9 and 15, six letters were exchanged between Hertzog and Erasmus, and on February 16 the entire correspondence was published in the press.[15] The points developed in this correspondence may be summarized as follows:

Erasmus: Will the sovereign independence of South Africa, the divisibility of the Crown, and the Union's right to neutrality and secession from the Empire be set out clearly in the program of the new party?

Hertzog: No. Any such statement would confuse rather than clarify and might suggest doubts as to the Union's true constitutional position. Hertzog stated, however, his personal conviction that the Union was a sovereign and independent state, that the Crown was divisible, and that South Africa had the right to neutrality in any war involving Great Britain and to secession from the British Commonwealth.

Erasmus: Will members of the new party have the right to make propaganda for a republic?

Hertzog: Yes, or for any other form of government.

Erasmus: Will the Prime Minister recommend the appointment of a South African as the next Governor-General?

Hertzog: Yes, if there is popular demand for such an appointment.

Erasmus: Is the Prime Minister willing to abolish the right of appeal to the Privy Council, to alter the present nationality laws so as to make South African nationality consistent with the independent status of the Union, and to eliminate other constitutional "anomalies"?

Hertzog: Consideration is now being given to abolition of appeals to the Privy Council and to other such problems.

Publication of the Hertzog-Erasmus correspondence in the middle of February appeared to end division within the

[14]Pirow, *James Barry Munnik Hertzog*, pp. 171-172.
[15]See, for example, *The Cape Times*.

National Party. Hertzog shortly addressed a message to his followers calling upon them "to bring about, together with this unity, also the peace and wholehearted cooperation which in the past were such a power in our party,"[16] and Malan expressed similar sentiments. But now the ranks of the South African Party were agitated, for the public gained the impression that the Hertzog-Erasmus agreements defined the program of the proposed new party.

In fact, discussions concerning the new party that had been going on between Smuts and Hertzog since December were still proceeding. To demonstrate that the Hertzog-Erasmus letters were a domestic matter of the National Party, Smuts wrote to Hertzog on February 18 pointing out that he could not agree with Hertzog's contention that inherent in the Union's independent status were the conceptions of the divisibility of the Crown, neutrality, and secession. "I assume," Smuts stated, "that these are matters of interpretation on which we differ and have differed, and that they are not matters on which we are called upon to come to an agreement in drawing up a programme of principles." Smuts went on to say that he could not agree to the inclusion in the program of the new party of any commitment to a substantial modification of the Union's nationality laws, and that while he did not wish to limit the freedom of expression of party members on constitutional issues, he considered it necessary that the party program declare support for the maintenance of the existing constitutional position. The centrality of the issue of national independence in these discussions was thus reemphasized. More important, in the light of the war vote five years hence, Smuts conceded in 1934 that political cooperation between Afrikaner nationalists and British South Africans was possible only if agreement on the issues of the divisibility of the Crown, neutrality, and secession was not required. In his immediate written response to Smuts, Hertzog accepted all of these points and this exchange of letters was also published in the press.[17]

[16]Leslie Blackwell, *African Occasions: Reminiscences of Thirty Years of Bar, Bench and Politics in South Africa* (London: Hutchinson, 1938), p. 238.
[17]See, for example, *The Cape Times,* February 19, 1934.

In the eyes of the Malanite faction of the National Party, the contents of Hertzog's correspondence with Smuts proved the duplicity of the Prime Minister. Despite his recent assurances to Malan and Erasmus, Hertzog appeared willing to abandon the principles of the National Party, or at least not to insist on them, as the price of Fusion. Speaking at Piet Retief in the eastern Transvaal on February 22, Malan stated: "The events of the last few days have definitely killed fusion."[18] Thereafter, the relationship between Malan and Hertzog worsened from day to day. Assisted by much of the Party press, the Malanite section of the National Party was henceforth uncompromising in its opposition to union with Smuts.

April 23 brought agreement between Hertzog and Smuts on a preliminary draft of the terms of Fusion.[19] The agreement began with a reaffirmation of the "seven points" on which the coalition had been based, but it was now stated that separate parliamentary representation might be provided for Africans. Predictably, national independence was a dominant issue. The Fusion agreement stated that the new government would maintain the existing Commonwealth relationship on the understanding that South Africa would assume no external obligations in conflict with "her own interests," but except for a statement that South African policy would be guided by the principle of "South Africa first," the nature of these "interests" was not spelled out. In particular, South Africa's stake in a united Commonwealth in time of war went unexplored. Individuals were left free to interpret the divisibility of the Crown differently, and it was clear from the April debate on the Status of Union Bill in Parliament that they did.

The final act to the year-long drama began on June 20 when the Union Head Committee of the South African Party and the Federal Council of the National Party considered separately the draft program for the new party at the Union Buildings in Pretoria. The South African Party had little

[18]*The Cape Times,* February 24, 1934.
[19]On June 6, the proposed terms of Fusion were set out in the press. See, for example, *The Cape Times.*

difficulty in deciding to accept the draft program, although Colonel C. F. Stallard stood apart.[20] The meeting of the Federal Council proved more contentious, however, and lasted into the following morning before a decision was reached. Not surprisingly, opposition to the draft principles of Fusion in the Federal Council came from the supporters of Malan. When the final vote was taken on a motion to accept the principles and recommend them to the various provincial congresses of the party, the Malan forces were defeated 13 to 7. Malan then read to the Federal Council the following statement: "The Head Committee has instructed the representatives of the Cape Province that, in case matters developed as they have now done, they should inform the Federal Council that it had been decided to recommend to the next Congress of the Nationalist Party in the Cape that the accepted basis be rejected and that the Nationalist Party shall continue to exist."[21] Later that day, the Malan group issued a statement setting forth their objections to the action taken by the Federal Council. The statement claimed that the council had been presented with an accomplished fact because it had not been possible to amend the draft principles prepared by Hertzog and Smuts. In particular, it complained that the terms of Fusion failed to include a definitive statement of South African sovereign independence, and in expressing a wish for the maintenance of the existing Commonwealth relationship, it hampered "future constitutional development." After a listing of other grievances, most being of an economic character, the statement concluded by calling for a policy of strict South African neutrality, and for a party that would be a "people's party and not machine controlled."[22]

After the events of June 20-21, the meetings of the provincial congresses of the National Party in July and August were anticlimatic. Although a meeting of MP's and Provincial Councilors from the Cape decided in favor of Fusion at De

[20]*The Cape Times,* June 22, 1934.
[21]*The Star,* June 21, 1934.
[22]*The Cape Times,* June 22, 1934.

Aar on July 5,[23] the pro-Fusion forces at the meeting of the Cape congress on July 25 at Somerset West were greatly outnumbered, and a motion rejecting Fusion was accepted, 164 to 18.[24] At the Free State congress at Bloemfontein on July 31, it was the anti-Fusion forces that were in the minority; Fusion was accepted by the Free State Nationalists, 107 to 27.[25] The 27 dissidents promptly retired to the Oranje-Koffiehuis where they resolved to continue the existence of the National Party in that province.[26] Fusion was accepted 281 to 38 by the Transvaal congress meeting in Pretoria in August, and in this instance the minority immediately gathered in the Polley's Hotel and decided to perpetuate the National Party in the Transvaal.[27] The Natal congress accepted Fusion without incident. Also in August, Fusion was accepted by a national congress of the South African Party in Bloemfontein over limited but resolute opposition led by Stallard.[28] He soon set about organizing the Dominion Party of South Africa for the defense of imperial interests in the Union, and at the opening of the next parliamentary session, three other MP's joined Stallard on the opposition benches.

Meanwhile, the dissident Nationalists reconstituted at the national level what remained of their party, renaming it the Purified National Party (Gesuiwerde Nasionale Party), the GNP. Of the 75 Nationalist MP's elected in 1933, 19 shunned Fusion and joined the GNP: 1 of 32 from the Transvaal, 4 of 15 from the Free State, and 14 of 27 from the Cape Province. At the opening of Parliament in January 1935, the GNP was the largest of the opposition groups and Malan was formally designated Leader of the Opposition. Finally, the two great parties, each now freed of its dissident wing, came together at Bloemfontein on December 5 to place the

[23]*The Cape Times,* July 6, 1934.
[24]*The Cape Times,* July 26, 1934.
[25]*The Cape Times,* August 1, 1934.
[26]Jannie Kruger, *President C. R. Swart* (Johannesburg: Nasionale Boekhandel, 1961), p. 97.
[27]Gert Coetsee, *Hans Strijdom: Lewensloop en Beleid van Suid-Afrika se Vyfde Premier* (Cape Town: Tafelberg-Uitgewers, 1958), p. 22.
[28]Blackwell, *African Occasions,* p. 258.

seal on Fusion. The United South African National Party, later referred to as the United Party, UP, was born.

In Retrospect

After the final break in June between the Hertzogites and the Malanites, each group attempted to lay the responsibility for the political schism in the National Party at the feet of the other. Hertzog and his followers accused Malan of bad faith, political trickery, and "racialism." Malan, Hertzog claimed, had "capitulated to a small band of political extremists." "No party in this country," the Prime Minister stated, "can be built upon a foundation of hate towards its fellow citizens simply because they are English-speaking. The cleavage they have created is a racial cleavage, devoid of principle."[29] For his part, Malan accused Hertzog of breaking his word to the Cape Head Committee and selling out the principles of the National Party. Inevitably, there was much hyperbole but some truth in both allegations.

In 1934, both Hertzog and Malan were committed to the ideal of a political party wherein all white South Africans sharing the same political convictions might be at home. Both were agreed, moreover, that the partisan divisions then existing in the Union fell short of this ideal. Differences between the two men developed on the means whereby such a party might be brought into being and on the content of the policies to which such a party would be committed. Shorn of semantic quibbles, what Malan proposed was to keep the National Party in substantially its existing form while inviting members of the South African Party to join it. Hertzog, in contrast, proposed a new party, founded on the basis of principles drawn up by himself and Smuts and in which membership would be open to all persons who subscribed to these principles. Negotiations between the two foundered on the issue of the specific constitutional provisos regarding South Africa's relations with Great Britain and the British Commonwealth to be included in the program of the new party. Agreement with Smuts and the South African Party

[29]*The Cape Times,* August 2, 1934.

required of Hertzog that he soften his own constitutional demands. Moreover, although points of constitutional difference were still outstanding between Hertzog and Smuts in 1934, since 1926 Hertzog had moved toward Smuts and hence away from the ardently republican wing of the National Party in his interpretation of the Union's constitutional position. But Malan had remained republican to the core, and drawing strength from his political colleagues in the Cape, he could be satisfied with nothing less than explicit constitutional exactitude. These differences, exaggerated by the often petty insistence of Malan and the Cape Head Committee on details, and a certain posture of arrogance and condescension assumed by the Prime Minister during the deliberations, brought to naught efforts to reconcile Hertzog and the Cape Nationalists.

But these disagreements on constitutional issues were symptoms of an even deeper cleavage. At its root, Afrikaner nationalism was both republican *and* culturally isolationist, and the National Party, whose founding this nationalism inspired and thereafter sustained, necessarily shared these attitudes. In 1912, Hertzog feared that Botha's policy of "conciliation" was out a euphemism for an open competition between the Afrikaner and the British ways of life, with the weaker one destined to disappear. Believing that the cultural values of his simple, rural people could not withstand the pressure of the older, richer, and more powerful British tradition, Hertzog called for a cultural segregation within the white population of South Africa, the so-called "two-stream" concept. In the late 1920s and 1930s, however, Hertzog revised his belief in the need for a separation of the two white language groups. On the one hand, he now possessed new confidence in the capacity of the Afrikaner to stand on the basis of equality with his fellow English South Africans, while on the other, he perceived that many English South Africans had come to place their first loyalty in South Africa — had become, as it were, English-speaking Afrikaners. Moreover, Hertzog saw that the country faced problems in which both Afrikaners and English South Africans shared a common interest, and he believed that these problems could be settled most effectively through political cooperation across ethnic lines.

But Hertzog's change of outlook had run ahead of sentiment within a considerable segment of the National Party. The Malanites especially did not believe that Hertzog's "integrative" approach to white unity in South Africa was at all possible. They wholly rejected Hertzog's belief in the readiness of English South Africans to embrace the Union as their fatherland in the same manner as the Afrikaner. The working out of the "two-stream" concept had, indeed, raised the Afrikaner to equal standing with his English-speaking fellow citizens, but in the eyes of the followers of Malan, this process had left unaffected the attachment of English South Africans to values and institutions alien to the country. Unlike Hertzog, Malan could see no evidence of a change in the nature of the English-speaking population, and, moreover, he was deeply suspicious of the willingness of Smuts to unite with Hertzog, vaguely seeing some treacherous motive beneath Smuts' sanguine pronouncements on national unity. From Malan's standpoint, the English South African would never voluntarily relinquish his un-Afrikaner associations with Great Britain; he would remain, until persuaded or compelled to change, an "unassimilated" element in the white population of the Union. The Malanites preferred persuasion, "but they were not sufficiently optimistic or convinced of their inherent strength to believe that persuasion would have much effect until the English had been brought face to face with the other alternative."[30]

By 1934, Hertzog believed it was possible through the processes of integration and compromise to merge the life styles of the Afrikaner and English-speaking communities and create a single and unified white South African nation. Malan denied this; in a context of competing sets of national values, unity could be achieved only by the domination of one or the other, and the only assurance that the Afrikaner's conceptions of the nation would triumph lay in the solidarity

[30]Michael Roberts and A. E. G. Trollip, *The South African Opposition, 1939-1945: An Essay in Contemporary History* (Cape Town: Longmans, Green, 1947), p. 15.

of the Afrikaner majority in the white population. For Malan there thus could be no question of union *(vereniging)* between Nationalists and others not yet imbued with the same inner convictions. *Vereniging* would erode both the principles and the political power of the Afrikaner. The task of the National Party should be, rather, the consolidation *(hereniging)* of the Afrikaner community so as to better force upon the English-speaking South African the realization that if he was ever to count in South Africa, he would have to become at one in national spirit, if not necessarily in language, with the Afrikaner. Hertzog had broken the growing unity of the Afrikaans-speaking community in leading a majority of the National Party into Fusion; Malan must now work to reestablish this unity. For his attitude, Hertzog termed Malan a "racialist," but the Cape leader could have no real objection to this, for the essence of his position was that the "racial" cleavage, dividing the true South African from the alien, was the only honest political division.

This attitude was in some measure present among Afrikaners throughout South Africa, although in the Transvaal the number of individuals of such a mind was indeed small, perhaps because in the rural areas of the Transvaal, "union" amounted to local "consolidation" of the Afrikaans-speaking community. In the Free State, the Malanite faction was sizable within the National Party, for here the unity of the Volk had already been achieved under the aegis of the Nationalists. But in the Free State the opponents of Fusion had to contend with the great personal following enjoyed by Hertzog, against whom they could not hope to capture control of the provincial organization. Only in the Cape Province did the opponents of Fusion have control of the National Party's organization. It was this control which allowed the anti-Fusion forces to deny Hertzog the support of the Cape National Party in 1934, even in the face of some popular support for the union of the two great parties, including that of nearly half the number of Cape Nationalist MP's.

3.

Right Versus Center

DISCUSSING "tensions in South Africa" in the 1930s, Nicholas Mansergh wrote in 1951:

> Outside of the field of Native policy, party fusion did not make for a strong government. In all controversial issues at home the policy of the Fusion government was of letting sleeping dogs lie. Differences had been papered over, not resolved; and the unassailable majority of the Fusion government in the House of Assembly was no true criterion of its strength. Progress was by agreement between those who on many issues were in fundamental disagreement, and the result was little progress. With that white South Africa as a whole was well content. Fusion had been made possible by a deep desire for internal peace and it was not inaction, but imprudent action, that was likely to bring back party warfare with all its fruitless asperities. Because of a continuing anxiety for party peace it was not, therefore, from within but from without that the most dangerous challenges to this experiment in racial co-operation were likely to come.[1]

Yet from the standpoint of the "conciliation" of Afrikaners and English South Africans, at least, the promise of Fusion was not that it would provide strong government. As Mansergh suggests, the compromises needed to effect Fusion

[1]Nicholas Mansergh, *Survey of British Commonwealth Affairs: Problems of External Policy, 1931-1939* (London: Oxford University Press, 1952), p. 230.

necessarily precluded strong government in most subject areas. The promise of Fusion was, rather, that the new government would be able to provide political shelter and encouragement for the manifold, but essentially nonpolitical stimulants to national (white) integration. To be successful in these terms, government had to be not so much strong as stable, for the process of integration is slow acting. Thus in the middle 1930s, the question was not the strength of the new United Party government but its durability. Did the United Party enjoy the same degree of public support that it possessed in Parliament, and could the government withstand for long the inevitable pressures that would be mounted against it by the "purified" Nationalists? This chapter suggests that Fusion was a popular as well as a parliamentary event, and that within the terms of the Fusion agreement, the partisan realignments of 1934 were lasting. We shall explore these matters through an examination of the activities and subsequent electoral success of the "purified" National Party between 1934 and the general election of 1938.

Party Organization

From the standpoint of party organization, Fusion was a disaster for the "purified" Nationalists, and for several years thereafter their party was a regional rather than a national political body.[2] The GNP was strongest in the Cape Province, for despite the fact that 13 of 27 Nationalist MP's from the Cape followed Hertzog into the United Party, Malan succeed-

[2]The structure of the GNP, on paper at least, was similar to the structure of the National Party under Hertzog, and, indeed, this pattern of organization was continued by successor parties to the GNP. At the Union level the party was a federation of provincial organizations, and in principle these provincial bodies enjoyed considerable autonomy, each having its own constitution. Within each province, policy-making authority rested with the annual provincial congress consisting of delegates from divisional committees or, in the case of the Transvaal, local branches of the party. The Federal Council, consisting of equal representation from each province, was charged with keeping the provincial organizations in touch with each other and with responsibility for propaganda and press relations. True coordinating power, however, was exercised by the leadership of the party's parliamentary caucus.

ed in salvaging most of the National Party's provincial
organization. Well before the final break with Hertzog, the
Cape provincial secretary, F. C. Erasmus, had worked to
establish the loyalty of the Cape organization of the National
Party to the provincial leader, rather than to the national
leader. The Nationalist press in the Cape Province similarly
stood by Malan, despite a serious challenge for its control
put forward by supporters of Hertzog. Malan thus had the
support of *Die Burger,* a Cape Town daily newspaper, and
its publishing house, Die Nasionale Pers, which since their
founding in 1915 had faithfully served the Cape National
Party.[3]

In Natal, Fusion virtually eliminated the National Party
from the province, and for many years the GNP existed in
Natal in name only. The position in the Transvaal seemed
initially as bad. Fusion saw nearly the entire National Party
in the Transvaal enthusiastically join hands with the followers of Smuts. The "purified" Nationalists thus began in the
Transvaal with few of the requisites of successful political
organization. The party had no press until October 1937, when
Die Transvaler was established as a daily newpaper in Johannesburg, and it had little money. During the party's early
years, J. G. Strijdom, the sole Nationalist MP in the Transvaal, covered the provincial expenses of the GNP with considerable amounts of his personal funds. Indeed, the Transvaal
GNP could not afford to hire full-time, paid officials until
the early 1940s.[4] Nor did the party have popular leaders. As
the only spokesman in the House of Assembly, party leadership in the Transvaal inevitably came to be lodged in Strijdom, but until Fusion he had been a little known backbencher.
Finally, the GNP had little organization at the outset apart
from Strijdom's own Waterberg constituency, and even in
Waterberg several branches of the National Party voted to
support Fusion. Only in 1936 did the outline of a provincial
organization begin to emerge in the Transvaal.

In the Free State the position of the "purified" Nationalists
was not so precarious. The initial reaction of Free State

[3]Malan was the first editor of *Die Burger.* He was editor until 1924.
[4]Coetsee, *Strijdom,* pp. 23, 28.

Nationalists in 1933 to the idea of Fusion with Smuts was not particularly enthusiastic, but the Free State was also the home ground of Hertzog, and in the end the Prime Minister's influence had been sufficient to take all but a minority of the Free State National Party with him. That minority, however, was no impotent political group. They had the support of the National Party organ in the Free State, *Die Volksblad,* a Bloemfontein affiliate of Die Nasionale Pers, and their leader N.J. van der Merwe, was well known and popular. The GNP in the Free State held four seats in the House of Assembly. These MP's were comparatively young men, but they were politically experienced, shrewd, and tireless workers, and in their home constituencies they were politically entrenched. While the "purified" National Party in the Free State could not match the United Party in organization, funds, or in the prestige of its leadership, neither could it be easily overwhelmed.

Issues

In the course of their 1964 summary of scholarly work on the integration of political communities, Philip Jacob and Henry Teune identified ten factors that contribute to the achievement of political integration.[5] These perhaps can be summarized as (a) those factors that increase social homogeneity, (b) those that increase social interdependence, and (c) those that increase mutual sympathy among members of society. Continuing the discussion begun in the Introduction, it is clear that it was both a long-term goal and a short-term electoral strategy of the United Party, as a party of conciliation, to foster — by example, appeals, policies, and inducements — greater homogeneity, interdependence, and mutual sympathy between Afrikaners and English-speaking persons. And conversely, it was inevitable that the goal of the "purified" National Party of preserving and protecting Afrikaner nationalism should cause it to try to prevent such political integration from occurring. As a political party in opposition, there were limits to the opportunities open to the GNP to impede the political integration of Afrikaners and English

[5]Jacob and Teune, "The Integrative Process," pp. 16-45.

South Africans. (Indeed, as we have suggested, while it is doubtless true that the exercise of political power can affect the pace of political integration, it is also the case that the process is greatly affected by innumerable events and changes in society — such as urbanization, media growth, and industrialization — that cannot be fully controlled even by those with political power.) In the middle of the 1930s the "purified" Nationalists focused their attentions on undermining the confidence of Afrikaners in the Fusion experiment and hence lessening mutual sympathy between the two white language groups.

But although the defection of the "purified" Nationalists left former Nationalists a minority in the parliamentary caucus of the new United Party, this did not deter Hertzog from holding to the same policies he had previously followed. The United Party consequently left little to be desired by most Afrikaners, save for the most incorrigible opponents of Fusion. Nevertheless, the Nationalists persisted in maintaining that the Fusion agreement had compromised the principles of the former National Party, and they asserted that the GNP was now the only available instrument for the realization and defense of these principles — for example, independence of the Union, protection of "white civilization," and the social and economic uplift of the Afrikaner. Concurrently, the Nationalists sought to intensify the more general spirit of nationalism among Afrikaners that gave these principles their particular significance. It was an obvious and necessary strategy, but because of the command of the United Party over the center in white South African politics, the "purified" Nationalists in Parliament were driven to adopt ever more narrow, isolationist, and reactionary attitudes.

The emergence of explicit anti-Semitism in Nationalist thinking in the late 1930s illustrates this reaction. Until then, anti-Semitism had not been characteristic of the Afrikaner. Indeed, the Jewish trader had been an accepted figure in South African rural life as early as the years of the republics. Afrikaners could see their own history as similar to that of the Old Testament Hebrews, and in consequence they experienced a fellow-feeling for the Jews. But by the middle of the 1930s this perspective gradually broke down in response to currents of anti-Semitism sweeping Europe and a marked increase in Jewish immigration to the Union. As the Jewish population increased, so, too, did agitation against Jews, "especially in the dorps and smaller towns, which were full of disappointed Afrikaners who had been driven off the land and were dismayed to find urban trade and industry so largely in the hands of foreigners."[6] Here was a chance both to promote and to exploit feelings of comparative class deprivation among Afrikaners. In 1936 the "purified" National Party opposed further Jewish immigration to the Union and defended this position with arguments that tended to indict not only Jewish immigrants but Jews already in the country, and a year later the GNP in the Transvaal officially excluded Jews from membership. E.S. Sachs notes that also in 1937 the national secretary of the GNP thanked Louis Weichardt, founder of the inconsequential but virulently anti-Semitic Grey Shirts organization, for "drawing the attention of the people to the Jewish problem, which has indeed assumed very threatening dimensions," and Sachs records that at the general election of 1938, electoral pacts were formed between the Nationalists and the Grey Shirts in several constituencies.[7]

But while the policy of the GNP was at first highlighted by special pleading for the interests of the economically downtrodden Afrikaner, the "have-nots," and those aggrieved by the administration of the economy — together with a restatement of traditional Afrikaner hostility towards so-called "British capitalism and Imperialism" — the value of this appeal was markedly reduced when the number of such persons appreciably declined in the middle 1930s as South Africa passed into a period of unprecedented prosperity. It was thus not long before constitutional and related issues returned as the heart of the Nationalist challenge to the United Party as Malan sought to undo Fusion by calling into question the independence of the Union. For example, in 1935 the Nationalists professed themselves shocked at the

[6]Walker, *A History of Southern Africa,* p. 655.
[7]E. S. (Solly) Sachs, *Rebels Daughters* (Great Britain: MacGibbon and Key, 1957), p. 131.

presence of a British admiral in the train of the Governor-General at the opening of Parliament, called again for the abolition of the right of appeal to the Privy Council, and assailed the status of South Africans as both British subjects and Union nationals as being constitutionally anomalous. Speaking to the Cape congress of the National Party at Worcester in September 1936, Malan insisted that South Africa have one citizenship, one flag, and a single national anthem.[8] "Intergrative" solutions to value conflict situations between Afrikaners and British South Africans were thus held to be unsatisfactory.

The question of the Union's national anthem became a heated issue in 1938 and aptly illustrates the limitations of an "integrative" approach to resolving conflict where consummatory values are involved. Before 1938, "God Save the King" had been widely regarded as the national anthem of the Union, but at the opening of Parliament in 1938, Hertzog personally ordered the playing of "God Save the King" *and* "Die Stem van Suid-Afrika" ("The Voice of South Africa"), a moving, patriotic song that had been gaining increasing recognition from Afrikaners, many of whom felt no attachment to "God Save the King." Several English-speaking MP's immediately challenged the propriety of the Prime Minister's action, which prompted Hertzog to say that the Union had no single national anthem that was generally accepted or officially recognized. Hertzog characterized "God Save the King" as only a "solemn invocation to the Almighty for His protection to our King," and he said that it would continue to be played on all "appropriate occasions." But at such times, he continued, "Die Stem" would also be played in recognition of the "special esteem" in which it was held by very many Afrikaners. This result seemed to satisfy few besides Hertzog. The Dominion Party complained that Hertzog had diminished the standing of "God Save the King," a position with which many English-speaking MP's appear to have agreed, while the Nationalists suggested that the Prime Minister was unwilling to recognize "Die Stem" as anything more than

[8]*The Cape Times,* October 1, 1936.

a popular Afrikaans folksong. On March 19, 1938, N.J. van
der Merwe complained in Parliament that the Prime Minister
was willing to speak of "Die Stem" as "a thing for the
Afrikaans-speaking people." "It is our object," van der Merwe
claimed, "to get one national anthem for South Africa."[9] As
a general proposition, it seems that there is something vaguely
unsatisfying about arrangements that give equal standing to
social objects, some of which are endowed by the viewer with
consummatory significance, and some of which are not.

But most of all, the Nationalists returned again and again
to the twin issues of neutrality and secession, seeking to expose
divisions within the United Party on these matters and depict
the government as an unreliable guardian of the Union's
sovereignty. Here was the United Party's Achilles' heel, for
as we have already noted, cooperation between Hertzog and
Smuts in 1934 was possible because — there being no current
need for action — they could agree to disagree on the questions
of neutrality and secession. The "purified" Nationalists supported Hertzog in his belief that South Africa had a right
to be neutral in any war involving Britain and might secede
from the British Commonwealth if it desired, but they repeatedly accused him of being a captive of a party that did
not entirely share these views and of aligning South Africa
in ways that would make it difficult for the Union to exercise
its rights in practice. Malan claimed, for example, that
Hertzog's association of South Africa with plans for the
defense of colonial territories to the north of the Union
"carried the implication of joint defense cooperation with the
country [Britain] whose territories they were."[10]

After 1934, nearly all Nationalists were republicans. Because of this, as well as frustration due to continuing uncertainty on the questions of neutrality and secession, public
insistence of the "purified" National Party on the right of
South Africa to secede from the Commonwealth shortly
shifted to public advocacy of such secession. N.J. van der
Merwe seems to have expressed the sentiments of all Nationalists when in parliamentary debate on the 1937 Coronation

[9]*House of Assembly Debates,* Vol. 31, 1938, cols 286, 298, and 1646.
[10]Mansergh, *Survey of British Commonwealth Affairs,* p. 239.

Oath Bill he declared: "I must frankly say that whether the Crown is already divided or not divided, whether it is divisible or indivisible, is to my mind an absurdity, and the sooner we get rid of the institution the better."[11]

By the end of 1936, all four provincial branches of the GNP were committed to the creation of a republic, although it was stated that this might come about only "on the broad basis of the will of the people," specially expressed.[12] This meant a special referendum, not just a majority vote in Parliament or a general election. Thereafter, Nationalists in Parliament lost no chance to demonstrate their republican zeal. The espousal of republicanism clouded somewhat the challenge of the National Party to the government on the issues of neutrality and secession. Moreover, it doubtless lost the party the support of some of those Afrikaners who while strong for national independence, were not yet ready to abandon the Monarchy. Republicanism established, however, an unambiguous, substantive difference between the "purified" National Party and the United Party which could guarantee political survival, if not electoral success. In 1936, Malan could not ignore the value of such insurance.

Nationalism Resurgent

From its founding in 1914, the success of the National Party of Hertzog was linked to the presence of three conditions: the fact that Afrikaners were a majority in the South African electorate; Afrikaner nationalism; and the acceptance by Afrikaner nationalists of the self-appointed role of the National Party as the only proper represenative in politics of the Afrikaner Volk. In fact, the second and third of these conditions were interrelated, for it appears that the more nationalist an Afrikaner was, the more likely he was to feel that Afrikaners ought to remain politically independent of non-Afrikaners. Expressed in different words, if an Afrikaner regarded the fact of being an Afrikaner as a consummatory value, he was unlikely to find the compromises required for

[11]*House of Assembly Debates,* Vol. 28, 1937, col. 1151.
[12]G. D. Scholtz, *Dr. Nicholaas Johannes van der Merwe, 1888-1940* (Johannesburg: Voortrekkerpers, 1944), pp. 300-301, 304-305.

political union with British South Africans to be acceptable. Early in 1934, when the idea of a union between Hertzog and Smuts was dividing the National Party, this association between the ideas of Afrikaner nationalism and Afrikaner political isolation was eloquently put in a joint statement by four Nationalist MP's that appeared in *Die Volksblad* on January 13: "For us, the National Party was and is always more than a mere political party; it is a movement born from the heart of the Volk which joins everything which is precious in our Volk-history and can serve as the only guiding principle in the glorious work of building [our] nation."

After 1934, these same conditions were no less important for the "purified" National Party. Indeed, Malan's support for the removal of Africans from the common voters' roll in the Cape Province in 1936 and his urging that Coloured voters be removed as well can be seen, in part, as an effort to increase the proportion of Afrikaners in the electorate. Thus while it was a necessary strategy of the "purified" Nationalists in the middle 1930s to try to show that Hertzog *had* sacrificed Afrikaner interests in agreeing to enter the United Party, it was no less obvious that they would "concentrate for the moment on the strengthening of Afrikanderdom by every possible means, and in every field of human endeavor."[13]

This effort necessarily allied the National Party with those cultural, economic, and other organizations that also sought to serve, sustain, or uplift the Afrikaans-speaking population. D.W. Kruger has noted that at the time of Fusion, Afrikaner intellectual and cultural circles which had supported Hertzog shifted that support to Malan, for "the Afrikaans cultural movement had by no means achieved all of its aims."[14] Indeed, Fusion in 1934 followed by only a few years the beginnings of a comprehensive, vigorous, and coordinated campaign involving a variety of avowedly Afrikaans cultural, educational, economic, religious, labor, *and* political bodies that was directed toward the building of a self-conscious and

[13]Roberts and Trollip, *The South African Opposition*, p. 15.
[14]Kruger, *Age of the Generals*, p. 180.

cohesive Afrikaner Volk. This campaign, which may only now be coming to an end, has been treated at length elsewhere,[15] and here we need only emphasize briefly the "new withdrawal of the Afrikaner people from the community as a whole" that was its central strategy and aspect.[16]

Most studies of the integrative process stress the impact on social cohesion of different patterns of associational memberships. Lewis Coser, for example, has written that plural societies "which are built on multiple affiliations tend to be 'sewn together' by multiple and multiform conflicts between groups in which the members' personalities are involved only segmentally." Alternately, according to James Coleman, "in the community which does not create in its members the potential for cross-pressures, individuals are consistent; groups of friends are of one mind; and organizations are unified — all the conflict is shifted to the level of the community itself."[17] Before the 1930s there existed in South Africa a number of organizations and bodies having a distinctive Afrikaner character and the limited purpose of serving only, or especially, the Afrikaans-speaking population — for example, the three Dutch Reformed Churches; the publishing firm of Die Nasionale Pers; and the Suid-Afrikaanse Akademie vir Wetenskap en Kuns (the South African Academy for Science and Arts). But the founding of these and other such bodies before 1930 was not part of a comprehensive plan for the creation of social and economic self-sufficiency for the Afrikaans-speaking community. After 1930, however, this motive gained prominence in the minds of many Afrikaner nationalists and lay behind the establishment of a succession of distinctively Afrikaner bodies, often rivaling established but non-Afrikaner bodies, covering a broad spectrum of activities. In 1930 the Afrikaans Taal-en-Kultuurvereniging,

---

[15]See especially Shelia Patterson, *The Last Trek: A Study of the Boer People and the Afrikaner Nation* (London: Routledge & Kegan Paul, 1957), Chapter IV.
[16]Gwendolen M. Carter, *The Politics of Inequality: South Africa since 1948* (New York: Frederick A. Praeger, 1958), p. 32.
[17]Lewis Coser, *The Functions of Social Conflict* (Glencoe: The Free Press, 1956), p. 80; James S. Coleman, *Community Conflict* (Glencoe: The Free Press, 1957), p. 22.

subsequently an important cultural organization among Afrikaner railwaymen, was founded. The next year the Voortrekker Movement was created as an Afrikaner equivalent of the Scouting movement, which was regarded to have been insufficiently "national-minded." In 1933 the student bodies at most Afrikaans-speaking universities withdrew from the National Union of South African Students in order to establish the Afrikaanse Nasionale Studentebond (Afrikaner National Students League), and in 1934 the savings bank Volkskas was founded to compete with such established firms as Barclays Bank and the Standard Bank of South Africa, both of which had their head offices in London. The year 1935 saw the establishment of the Noodhulpliga, an Afrikaner equivalent of the Red Cross. Dr. Theo Wassenaar, founder of the Noodhulpliga, explained the reason for its creation in a letter to *Die Transvaler* published on February 17, 1940: "The Boer nation wants its own organization in this sphere, an organization that, guided by love of its own people, shall in the first place have the interests of the Boer nation at heart."

At the end of the 1930s the drive for Afrikaner self-sufficiency — or autarchy — began to give a new and substantially unprecedented emphasis to harnessing Afrikaner capitalism. As a result, between 1939 and 1948 the number of Afrikaner enterprises rose from 3,170 to 13,047, according to figures compiled by the Afrikaans Handelsinstituut (Commerce Institute), a body established in 1942 to assist Afrikaner businessmen.[18] Many other examples of this campaign might be cited, but the point is already clear: the Afrikaner separatist movement, beginning in the 1930s, reduced the organizational cross-pressures to which Afrikaners were subject, increasing the likelihood that social conflict involving Afrikaners and non-Afrikaners would henceforth be seen by the former in "national" terms, that is, as bearing on the welfare of the Afrikaner community as a people. Afrikaner nationalism was consequently extended and intensified at the expense of both mutual sympathy between the two language groups and Afrikaner support for the "conciliation" of the United Party.

[18]*Sunday Times,* October 15, 1950.

Illustrating this, in 1943 E.G. Malherbe reported that a survey of the attitudes of students at four teacher-training colleges in the Transvaal revealed that the proportion of the students who did not believe in "racial cooperation" — that is, cooperation between Afrikaners and English South Africans — was highest at Afrikaans medium institutions (where Afrikaans is the sole language of instruction), while it was lowest at bilingual schools. Moreover, Malherbe found that "amongst the students in Afrikaans medium institutions a prejudice against 'racial' cooperation . . . [was] accompanied by a desire to use the school for the spreading of political propaganda."[19]

The Broederbond

Identities in personnel, financial interdependencies, structural linkages, and philosophical çompatablility among the various Afrikaner cultural, educational, economic, religious, labor, *and* political organizations in the 1930s served to unite these bodies in a coordinated and comprehensive campaign for a renewal of Afrikaner nationalism. They also suggested the existence of central planning and direction. Because the "purified" National Party was a totalitarian party — in the sense that it supported a social ideology that defined, in avowedly moral terms, a complete life style for its followers — one might have expected that the party itself would have organized as its auxiliaries such bodies as we have referred to and have subjected them to its direction. Such is the pattern of totalitarian parties, as Maurice Duverger points out.[20] But in fact, this did not happen, at least not directly, although the GNP did organize a youth branch, the Nasionale Jeugbond, in 1938. Rather, it is generally agreed by students of South African affairs that the campaign for the resurgence of Afrikaner nationalism in the 1930s was planned and directed by a little known body calling itself the Afrikaner Broederbond (Brothers' League).

Soon after its founding in 1918 (or, according to some, 1919),

[19]E. G. Malherbe, *The Bilingual School* (Johannesburg: Central News Agency, 1943), pp. 125-126.
[20]Maurice Duverger, *Political Parties: Their Organization and Activities in the Modern State* (London: Methuen, 1959), pp. 116f.

the Afrikaner Broederbond became a secret society. In consequence little factual information as to its purposes, members,
or activities has been available. Opponents of the
Broederbond, both Afrikaans and English-speaking, have
been numerous and outspoken about its alleged nature, but
their characterizations have been difficult to substantiate.
The 1951 report of a commission of inquiry into the Broederbond, appointed by the Dutch Reformed Churches, provides
some useful information,[21] but to 1948 the Broederbond itself
issued but one public statement. This was a defense of the
organization in response to a recent attack upon the body
by Prime Minister Smuts. Speaking to a Union congress of
the United Party on December 6, 1944, Smuts called the
Broederbond "a dangerous, cunning, political, Fascist organization,"[22] and a few days later the government required all
civil servants (including teachers) who belonged to the Broederbond to resign or be dismissed from the public service.
In a series of articles appearing in *Die Transvaler* in December
1944 and January 1945, the secretary of the Broederbond,
I.M. Lombard, tried to reassure the public about the organization.[23]

According to Lombard, the Broederbond "was born out
of the deep conviction that the Afrikaner nation was planted
in this country by the hand of God and is destined to continue
to exist as a nation with its own character and calling." Its
purpose was "the establishment of a healthy and progressive
unanimity among all Afrikaners who strive for the welfare
of the Afrikaner nation; the awakening of national self-assurance among Afrikaners and the inspiration of love for the
language, religion, traditions, country, and people; [and] the
promotion of all the interests of the Afrikaner people." Among
numerous specific goals cited by Lombard, the two foremost
were (a) the achievement of full independence for South
Africa, and (b) the elimination of the inferior position of

[21]*The Transactions of the 22nd Council of Churches,* Bloemfontein,
May 16, 1951, Addendum B.
[22]The United Party, *General Smuts' Speech at the Union Congress
of the United Party,* Bloemfontein, December 6, 1944.
[23]See *Die Transvaler,* December 14, 1944, and January 3, 1945.

Afrikaners and of Afrikaans. Lombard thus corroborated four points we have made concerning Afrikaner nationalism: its identification with sacred ends, its concern with Afrikaner unity, the priority importance of the value of national independence, and its associated feelings of the relative social deprivation of Afrikaners.

On the basis of further information supplied by Lombard and other available data,[24] there seems little doubt that during the period under review the Afrikaner Broederbond was a clandestine and elitest organization of about 2,500 strategically located "national-minded" Afrikaners, with teachers, civil servants, clergymen, politicians, and other professional men predominating. This body was founded on a narrow and exclusive definition of the Afrikaner Volk and was dedicated not only to promoting the interests of the Volk, as defined by the Broederbond, but also to securing the dominance of these interests in the public life of the Union. The activities of the Broederbond were directed toward infiltrating and controlling established Afrikaner institutions, especially the churches and the schools, and to promoting the creation of new "national-minded" institutions and agencies under its influence in those fields where no distinctively Afrikaner bodies had previously existed.

The relationship between the Broederbond and the GNP is not easily defined. Although Lombard denied that the Broederbond was concerned with "party-politics," it is clear that it enjoyed a special relationship with the GNP and later the "reunited" National party after 1940. Indeed, in a speech at Smithfield in November 1935, Prime Minister Hertzog critically observed: "There is no doubt that the secret Broederbond is nothing else but a purified Nationalist Party busy underground, and the Purified Nationalist Party is nothing but a secret Afrikaner Broederbond continuing its activities above ground."[25]

Except for Mr. Speaker E.G. Jansen, no prominent member of the United Party (or after 1940, the Afrikaner Party) is

[24]One source of information is Carter, *The Politics of Inequality,* pp. 251-258.
[25]*The Star,* November 7, 1935.

thought to have been a Broeder, but in contrast, the *Rand Daily Mail* alleged on May 20, 1948, that 60 of 92 Nationalist candidates in the general election of 1948 were members of the organization. There is no doubt that Malan, himself, Strijdom, Erasmus, and several other prominent "purified" Nationalists were members. It is too much to say, however, that the Broederbond controlled the GNP, or the reverse. Rather, it seems that the like-mindedness of the members, and especially of the leaders, of both organizations; the somewhat different preoccupations of the party and the Broederbond; and their overlapping memberships and interlocking directorates eliminated conflicts of interest and obviated any question of one being the superior to the other. Hertzog would appear to have been close to the truth when he stated in 1935 that both were merely different aspects of the same congregation.

Electoral Support

Because the life of the South African House of Assembly under the constitution is limited to a maximum of five years from its first sitting, a general election was required no later than May of 1938. Accordingly, the House was dissolved on April 11, 1938, and a general election was called for May 18. This was the first major test of the United Party's electoral support, although previous parliamentary by-elections and the provincial council elections of 1936 had (to no one's surprise) already identified the Orange Free State and the rural areas of the Cape Province as the strongholds of the Malanite Opposition.[26] Yet in the Free State, the most Afrikaans-speaking of the four provinces, the Nationalists in 1936 captured only 45 percent of the vote in the 23 seats they contested, even after "three years of intensive campaigning," according to the Bloemfontein *Friend*.[27] These Free State returns suggested that Malan had little chance of becoming prime minister unless his party could make a dramatic breakthrough to large numbers of Afrikaner voters. The 1938 election results confirmed the weakness of his position.

[26]*Round Table,* No. 102 (March 1936), p. 422.
[27]*The Friend,* September 11, 1936.

In the campaign of 1938 the government took its stand on the so-called "fruits of Fusion," with special emphasis placed on the economic health of the country. The Malanites responded by reiterating their positions on all the now familiar constitutional issues: neutrality, abolition of constitutional "anomalies," and the establishement of a republic. In particular, the Nationalists charged that the United Party could not be trusted not to drag South Africa into a European war.

In view of the supposed value of the "apartheid" issue to the anti-Smuts forces in 1948, it seems an important point that race issues were also highlighted in the campaign of 1938. In the middle of the decade the "purified" Nationalists had tried to characterize the Hertzog government as liberal in matters of race policy, but three major government measures at this time extending racial segregation in voting, in the ownership of land, and in the urban areas did a great deal to thwart this effort. Now in the 1938 campaign, the Nationalists tried again. Their manifesto insisted on the segregation of whites and nonwhites with respect to residential areas, trade unions, and places of work and demanded an end to African representation in Parliament and to the "wholesale buying of land for Natives."[28] Opposition spokesman returned continually to the race issue in the course of the campaign. They called for separate parlimentary representation for the Coloureds, job reservation by race, and an end to the employment of whites by nonwhites. Anticipating a similar charge ten years later, the Nationalists claimed that the United Party government was controlled by the Minister of the Interior, Public Health, and Education, Jan H. Hofmeyr, whose liberal attitudes on matters of race were well known. Particular attention was given to the government's refusal to outlaw racially mixed marriages. The Nationalists circulated a poster depicting the alleged evils of such marriages. This poster, called the *"baster plakkaat"* ("bastard poster"), showed a slovenly white woman relaxing with her too-smartly dressed African husband before their slum home, their two

[28]Federal Council of the National Party, *Election Manifesto of the National Party — General Election, 1938* (Cape Town, 1938).

Coloured children playing in the dust at their feet. The United Party claimed that the GNP had disparaged the honor of all white women in South Africa, and angry groups of white women demonstrated at several opposition election offices. In some cases the poster was quietly withdrawn by the local Nationalist candidate, but elsewhere, especially in the Free State, the opposition continued to insist that it properly represented the consequences of government policy.

This campaign of the National Party in 1938 was not notably successful. Although the GNP increased its representation from 20 to 27 seats, it gained little support outside the Free State and the rural Cape Province, and even there its strength seemed confined to areas of comparative economic deprivation. Laurence Salomon found that 17 of the 20 seats won by the GNP in the Cape Province in 1938 were located in areas where the 1932 percentage of white families in the Carnegie Commission's classification of the "very poor" was above the national average.[29] In the Transvaal, especially, the election was a disaster for Malan. There the Nationalists had made a serious bid for office and had been turned down nearly completely, receiving only 75,000 votes as against 185,000 cast for the United Party. Strijdom was returned from Waterberg, although with a majority smaller by half, but elsewhere the rout was complete. The party was particularly humiliated in its attempt to win the support of the Afrikaans-speaking working men in the Transvaal urban centers. Six months earlier *Round Table* surmised that the efforts of Nationalists to take over the Mine-workers' Union had driven the urban labor force into the arms of the government.[30]

1938 Election Results

United Party	111
National Party	27
Dominion Party	8
Labour Party	3
Independents	1

[29]Laurence Salomon, "Socio-Economic Aspects of Modern South African History, 1870-1962" (unpublished Ph.D. dissertation, Boston University, 1962), p. 67.
[30]*Round Table,* No. 109 (December 1937), p. 193.

Viewed nationally, the general election of 1938 established the "purified" National Party as the foremost opposition group but left it, nevertheless, a decided minority in the House of Assembly — a regional party without urban support. Even in the Cape and the Free State, Nationalists were in the minority. In the 103 constituencies that the "purified" National Party contested, the ratio of votes cast for its candidates as against those cast for all others stood at 100:132. Taking into account 47 constituencies that were without a Nationalist candidate in 1938, J.L. Grey calculated that 59.6 percent of all white, Afrikaans-speaking electors who had voted had supported Malan, and 40.4 percent had supported the United Party.[31]

Of the 1938 election, Malan later told his supporters: "In some ways we have been disappointed."[32] This sentiment is understandable. For over four years the Nationalists had vigorously pursued those strategies that the logic of their position dictated. They had repeatedly challenged the workability of the Fusion agreement, and they had worked sympathetically with others who were concerned to intensify and extend feelings of nationalism among Afrikaners. Yet in the end the party had secured the support of only six of every ten Afrikaner voters. Correctable organizational weaknesses were in part responsible for the dismal performance of the GNP in the Transvaal, a fact Malan himself recognized when soon after the election he said that it was in the Transvaal "where the future of our people and party lies."[33] Moreover, the resurgence of Afrikaner nationalism was clearly a long-term process whose political consequences might only emerge gradually over a number of years. Yet even allowing for such factors, the 1938 general election suggested the durability of the Fusion experiment. In 1929, at the height of its authority, the National Party of Hertzog had controlled 27 seats in the Cape Province and a majority of only 8 in the House

[31]J. L. Grey, "How the Nation Voted," *Common Sense,* August 1943. This article deals with the 1943 election, but comparisons are made with the 1938 election for which some figures are given.
[32]*The Star,* May 21, 1938.
[33]Coetsee, *Strijdom,* p. 26.

of Assembly. After the general election of 1938, the "purified" Nationalists controlled only 20 seats in the Cape, that province where Fusion had damaged them least. In the absence of any special circumstances, the United Party in 1938 captured nearly three-fourths of all the seats in the House of Assembly, an electoral victory that would remain unequalled until the Nationalists' landslide triumph of 1966. If the United Party's majority in Parliament was somewhat inflated, its long-term governing power seemed nonetheless secure. After 1938 there could be little doubt that the coming of Fusion had shifted more than a sufficient number of Afrikaner votes to keep Malan permanently in opposition so long as the United Party itself remained intact.

4.

End of Fusion

On Friday, September 1, 1939, Adolf Hitler's armies invaded Poland. Two days later, both Great Britain and France declared war on Germany. In South Africa, these events necessitated a decision on the issue of the Union's neutrality in a war involving Great Britain, that question on which Hertzog and Smuts could only agree to differ in 1934. This was a challenge to Fusion at its weakest point.

By an extraordinary coincidence, Parliament, normally in recess in September, was able to debate the Union's response to Britain's involvement in war immediately, for on September 2 Parliament had reconvened in order that the term of the Senate, soon to expire, might be extended. The cabinet met at Groote Schuur on the afternoon of September 2 to consider the war issue, and from the start it was clear that the government was hopelessly divided. Six ministers, including the Prime Minister, supported a declaration of neutrality, but seven others, led by Smuts, wanted an immediate declaration of war against Germany.[1] It was thus a divided government that met the House on the following Monday.

In a tense atmosphere on September 4, MP's heard the Prime Minister move approval of the statement that the "existing relations between the Union of South Africa and the various belligerant countries will, in so far as the Union is concerned, persist unchanged and continue as if no war is being waged."[2] Smuts countered with an amendment committing the Union to war against Hitler. The debate lasted

[1] *The Star,* September 4, 1939.
[2] *House of Assembly Debates,* Vol. 36, 1939, cols. 23-24.

all day until about 9 P.M. when the final division was taken. By a vote of 80 to 67, the House of Assembly resolved that the Union sever its relations with the German Reich and "refuse to adopt an attitude of neutrality" in the conflict between Great Britain and Germany.[3] Hertzog resigned his office the next day, after Governor-General Duncan refused his request to dissolve the House and call a general election, and on September 6 Smuts became Prime Minister for the second time. War was declared on Germany forthwith.

Smuts came to power in September 1939 with the assistance of four pre-1934 Nationalist MP's, and the new cabinet included six Afrikaners, three of whom were veterans of the Boer forces in the South African War. Nevertheless, the decision of September 4 stripped the United Party of all save a small vestige of its former Afrikaner support. Thereafter Hertzog said himself: "However we may regret what has occurred, there is no doubt that few other things could so quickly or effectively have consolidated Afrikaans-speaking Afrikanerdom."[4] A by-election at Kuruman in the Cape in 1940 suggested the striking political realignment that had occurred. In 1938, the United Party won at Kuruman with a majority of 714. In 1940, however, the seat was captured by the "reunited" National Party with a majority of 803, a shift in the vote of 14 percent. At the same time, English-speaking South Africans were virtually unanimous in support of the new government, which now was a coalition formed of the Labour Party and the Dominion Party together with

[3] *Ibid.*, cols. 24-31.
[4] van den Heever, *Hertzog,* p. 283. The results of five by-elections during the fifteen months following the 1938 election suggest that the United Party had lost some of its Afrikaans-speaking support even before the "war vote" of September 1939, and it is generally agreed that one event contributing to that loss was the Voortrekker Centenary celebrations which climaxed on December 16, 1938. Although the celebrations were organized ostensibly on non-political grounds, they were in fact soon captured by Afrikaner "extremists" who gave them a character that was often more 'nationalist' than 'national.' The Centenary celebrations thus had the effect of heightening an exclusive Afrikaner patriotism among the very many Afrikaners who participated. In context, this could only serve the political interests of Dr. Malan and the "purified" National Party. See Kruger, *Age of Generals,* p. 185.

the rump United Party. The "war vote" thus returned partisan alignments in South Africa to much the same pattern
that had prevailed in South Africa about 1929, although this
time Hertzog was out of power. As his biographer writes, "the
crisis had the effect of reuniting many of those Afrikaners
who had separated six years before."[5] Clearly, Fusion had
ended.

Smuts' thinking at this time merits special attention. A
year earlier, in September 1938, Smuts had agreed with other
members of the cabinet to a statement that had been prepared
by Hertzog setting forth the intention of the Union to remain
neutral in the event a major war should break out in Europe.[6]
This statement was substantially the same as Hertzog's
neutrality motion of September 1939. Oswald Pirow, among
others, later reproached Smuts for failing to give any notice
to Hertzog after September 1938 of his change of belief
regarding neutrality, but Smuts' "official" biographer, Sir
Keith Hancock, has shown the inaccuracy of this charge.[7]
Between October 1938 and August 1939, Smuts made at least
twenty well-publicized speeches concerning international developments and their significance for the Union. In these
speeches Smuts repeatedly made clear his own view that
Hancock has summarized in three linked propositions: South
Africa could not isolate herself, but needed friends; South
Africa's best friends were Britain and other nations of the
Commonwealth; and South Africa could not count on staying
neutral.[8] At the critical meeting of the cabinet on September
2, Smuts was warned by General J. C. G. Kemp that there
would be a "blood bath" in South Africa if the Union failed
to maintain neutrality, but this assessment was rejected by
Smuts.[9] There is no doubt, however, that the Deputy Prime
Minister recognized that to press the war issue in public would
split the United Party, terminate Fusion, and create bitter
divisions in the country. According to Hancock, "Smuts

[5]*Ibid.*, p. 284.
[6]W. K. Hancock, *Smuts, Vol. II: The Fields of Force, 1919-1950*
(Cambridge: Cambridge University Press, 1968), p. 285.
[7]Pirow, *Hertzog,* p. 242; Hancock, *Smuts,* Vol. II, pp. 315-317.
[8]Hancock, *Smuts,* Vol. II, p. 316.
[9]*Ibid.*, p. 319.

believed that the cleavage which Malan wanted and which Hertzog seemed to accept would do irreparable damage to the nation. He believed that the cleavage which he himself accepted could be repaired with time."[10]

But the "war vote" of 1939 not only terminated Fusion, it severely damaged the appeal of "conciliation" among Afrikaners. To be sure, thereafter Hertzog contended that Fusion had failed, not because it had been wrong in conception, but because of the perfidy of Smuts. To the followers of Malan, however, things seemed quite different. Hertzog had been mistaken in 1934, they thought; the principles of the Afrikaner Volk could not be served through cooperation with non-Afrikaners, at least not yet. Hertzog's defeat on September 4 was, they believed, proof of his earlier mistake, and the former Prime Minister should now confess to having made an error in judgment in 1934. But Hertzog showed no repentence. In a speech to his Smithfield constituents on November 4, 1939, he said: "Not only our national welfare and happiness, but our existence as a nation, depends on the measure of success in building up a united people from the two great sections of the community."[11] However, this position could no longer be maintained with political success among Afrikaners, as we shall see in the next chapter, and within a year Hertzog retired from politics.

If, therefore, "conciliation" were to continue as the policy of the government, it was necessary for Smuts to retain power without most of that support from the Afrikaans-speaking electorate that Fusion had brought in 1934. At least this would be necessary until such time as the process of national integration had commenced to bear fruit, and this was not likely to be soon. As Smuts himself wrote: "South Africa has a divided soul, but if we are faithful to the vision of forty years ago that soul will be one yet. Time is a causal factor and there has not yet been enough time. But in time it will come all right although we may not see it in our day."[12]

Smuts did, of course, defeat Hertzog in the House on Sep-

[10]*Ibid.*, p. 324.
[11]*The Star,* November 4, 1939.
[12]Hancock, *Smuts,* Vol. II, p. 324.

tember 4, but it seems possible that the vote in the House of Assembly on that day exaggerated the support Smuts had in the country. Hertzog said later that had the "purified" Nationalists accepted Fusion in 1934, he and not Smuts would have succeeded on September 4.[13] This was a reference to the fact that several former Nationalist constituencies returned Smuts candidates in 1938 because, the forces of Afrikanerdom being split, they had been able to defeat Hertzogites for the United Party nomination. And in December, *Round Table,* whose editors were certainly no partisans of Afrikaner nationalism, estimated that had a general election been held during the last quarter of 1939, it is probable that a majority of the voters would have supported Hertzog.[14] Indeed, there appears to have been a chance that Hertzog might have had the majority on September 4. Hancock reports that Hertzog himself was optimistic. But rather than limiting himself to the case for neutrality, Hertzog unwittingly defended Hitler in his speech in the House on September 4. This offended several MP's who had appeared to waiver, and they then sided with Smuts, placing the decision beyond Hertzog's reach.[15]

But whatever may have been the exact dimensions of Smuts' strength on September 6, 1939, there can be no doubt that the once secure position of the United Party had been lost. Between 1934 and 1939, South Africa could have been described as a one-party-dominant political system. There were at this time a number of parties, but the dominant position of the United Party was unassailable so long as the party itself remained united, and because of this, there was little doubt the country would continue to be committed to the policy of "conciliation." After September 1939, however, what was essentially a finely balanced two-party system reappeared. Thus even if it is accepted that the Smuts government could have been returned to power at a general election in the last quarter of 1939, its parliamentary majority

[13]Pirow, *Hertzog,* p. 255.
[14]*Round Table,* No. 117 (December 1939), 211.
[15]van den Heever, *Hertzog,* p. 282.

would certainly have been small, and had a later election coincided with even a minor reversal in public esteem, such a government was likely to be defeated. The lasting importance of the 1939 "war vote" for South African domestic politics was that it made it likely that in the future Afrikaner nationalists and proponents of "conciliation" would periodically alternate in and out of power as electoral support shifted first in favor of one group and then in favor of their opponents. At the least, such political discontinuity was certain to be damaging to the success of "conciliation" and the process of political integration which, as we have said, is slow to mature. Policies pursued by Smuts — for example, in public education or civil service recruitment — could be expected to be reversed when the Nationalists came to power, only to be reinstated at a later date. This would not only be detrimental to the success of the policies themselves, it would probably lead to public bitterness and frustration and to demands for changes in the political "rules of the game" to avoid such fluctuation.

Indeed, because after 1939 the United Party and the "reunited" Nationalists were fairly evenly divided electorally and differences between the two groups extended to the fundamental principles and values of South African society, it would seem possible to have predicted then that efforts would be made at an early date to alter the Union's electoral machinery to the permanent advantage of one side or the other. And as Smuts appeared less able to grasp fully the electoral realignment that had occurred in 1939, it was probable that it would be a Nationalist government that would recast the electoral system in their own interests.

I contend, albeit with the decided advantage of hindsight, that the major developments in South African politics over the three decades since the "war vote" of 1939 can be seen as the probable outcomes of that decision: the return to power of the Nationalists; their subsequent self-entrenchment in office; the end of "conciliation"; the transformation of South Africa into a republic; and the adoption of the principle of "separate development" as the official posture of white South

Africa toward nonwhite South Africa. In this view, Smuts risked the policy of "conciliation" and the future domestic politics of the Union in order that South Africa might contribute to the defeat of Hitler.

5.

1943: Electoral
Amplification

In his well known article, "A Theory of Critical Elections," published in 1955, the late V. O. Key, Jr., defined a "critical" election as one that manifests a sharp and durable partisan realignment within the electorate.[1] Five years later Angus Campbell and his three co-authors of *The American Voter* renamed Key's "critical" election a "realigning" election and further elaborated the concept, while concurrently extending Key's electoral typology to include two other election types.[2] As now understood, a "realigning" election has three interrelated characteristics: it occurs within a psychological context of intense public feeling, usually associated with some widely perceived, great national crisis; it results in a sharp realignment of a previously established voting pattern, and this change is subsequently seen to be lasting; following from this electoral realignment, the previous majority party in the country is defeated and a new majority party is established.

[1]V. O. Key, Jr., "A Theory of Critical Elections," *Journal of Politics*, XXVII, No. 1 (February 1955), 3.
[2]Angus Campbell, Philip E. Converse, Warren E. Miller, and Donald E. Stokes, *The American Voter* (New York: John Wiley & Sons, 1960), pp. 531-538. The two additional election types are a "maintaining" election, defined below in the text, and a "deviating" election, which is one where "the basic division of partisan loyalties is not seriously disturbed, but the attitude forces on the vote are such as to bring about the defeat of the majority party." More recently these same authors have suggested a fourth election type, covering the special case of a "maintaining" election that follows, and ends a period of electoral "deviation." Such an election they

Campbell and his co-authors are concerned only with American presidential elections, but there is no reason why the idea of a "realigning" election should not, when appropriate, be used to describe elections having these properties wherever they occur. The only prerequisite would seem to be that the political context be characterized by a stable and competitive two-party system and by partisan loyalties that tend to be lasting and durable.

In the 1940's, electoral politics in South Africa seemed to present such a context, and, indeed, the South African general election of May 26, 1948, is now widely understood to have been a "realigning" election, although different words are usually used to convey this meaning.[3] Gwendolen Carter, for example, writes that "1948 marks a watershed in South African politics," while Smuts' biographer, Sir Keith Hancock, has called the 1948 election the "most momentous" since Union.[4] For Leonard Thompson, the vote was "decisive," and John Cope quotes approvingly the words of Jan Hofmeyr, Smuts' deputy, when the final election figures were brought to him: "This is a revolution, not a political reverse."[5]

It is a fact, as we shall see, that compared with their showing

---

define as a "reinstating" election. This is one at which "the party enjoying a majority of party identifiers returns to power." (Philip E. Converse et al., "Stability and Change in 1960: A Reinstating Election," American Political Science Review, LV, No. 2, (June 1961), 280.) Taken together, these four categories provide a typology of elections wherein voting results are seen to reflect the interplay of two sets of forces. One set consists of stable, long-term partisan dispositions, the underlying division of partisan loyalties which define what a "normal" vote ought to be. The second set consists of changing, short-term attitude forces specific to the immediate electoral situation. These can deflect the vote away from its "normal" breakdown.

[3]South Africa had, of course, more than two parties during the 1940s, but except for the Afrikaner Party in 1948 (when it was allied with the National Party), none of the several "third" parties enjoyed important strength in the electorate. Thus for all practical purposes a two-party system obtained.

[4]Carter, The Politics of Inequality, p. 37; Hancock, Smuts, Vol. II, p. 506.

[5]Leonard M. Thompson, Politics in the Republic of South Africa (Boston: Little, Brown, 1966), p. 91; John Cope, South Africa (New York: Frederick A. Praeger, 1967), p. 123.

against the coalition government of Smuts at the previous general election in 1943, the National Party and the Afrikaner Party in alliance sharply increased their support in winning in 1948. Further, the partisan alignment shown in 1948 proved durable in the sense that government support increased steadily at each of the next four elections. And, of course, the 1948 election is best remembered for producing the opposition's campaign issue of race "apartheid." It is the commonplace conclusion that the opposition succeeded with this issue in awakening deep-seated fears among very many white voters, in effect manufacturing a great national crisis about South African race relations. Yet notwithstanding all of these points, I have argued elsewhere that the 1948 election, although doubtless a critical milestone in the evolution of South African policy, was not a "realigning" election according to the *full* definition of such an election that has been given above, and I continue to support this argument which is now repeated here.[6]

The issue is not so much the 1948 vote as the interpretation of the election five years earlier, for I believe that it is a general misunderstanding of the 1943 vote that has made a faulty view of 1948 not only common but practically inevitable. The 1943 election, which we will shortly describe at length, is widely understood, in the categories of *The American Voter,* to have been a "maintaining" election, that is, one at which the "pattern of partisan attachments prevailing in the preceding period persists and is the primary influence on forces governing the vote."[7] The essence of a "maintaining" election is that issues do not intrude to deflect the electorate from voting their standard, or normal, partisan allegiances. But I wish to contend below that while the pattern of continuing partisan attachments prevailing in the preceding period persisted in South Africa in 1943, "attitude forces" (to employ the language of *The American Voter*) that could be described as reinforcing, or *positive,* had the effect of

[6]Newell M. Stultz, "South Africa's 'Apartheid' Election of 1948 Reconsidered," *Plural Societies* (The Hague), III, No. 4 (Winter 1973), 25-38.
[7]Campbell *et al., The American Voter,* p. 531.

significantly *amplifying* Smuts' "normal" majority. Because
of this amplification in 1943, the realignment in basic partisan
attachments that came five years later appears more "sharp"
than in reality it was, and the role usually ascribed to
"apartheid" and the other attitude forces depressing Smuts'
majority in 1948, *negative* attitude forces as we shall call
them, is greater than it should be. Further, the long-range
contribution of the 1939 war vote is easily overlooked. In
this light, then, the 1948 election did not show the sudden,
sharp shift in long-run partisan voter identifications that is
said to be characteristic of "realigning" elections. The 1948
vote cannot be understood independent of the 1943 vote, but
the latter is poorly described as a "maintaining" election,
or indeed by any other of the electoral categories provided
by Angus Campbell and his associates. It seems necessary,
therefore, to propose a new category of elections, and accordingly I suggest that the election of 1943 was an "amplifying"
election in which *the basic division of partisan loyalties was
not seriously disturbed, but the attitude forces on the vote
were such as to increase appreciably the majority party's
"normal" margin of victory.*[8]

"Positive" Attitude Forces

Four short-term factors decreasing the appeal of the "reunited" National Party in 1943 can be identified. First, there
was the fact of party fission, the splitting of the party into
several bitterly warring factions beginning in late 1940. By
1943, 29 of the 67 MP's who had supported Hertzog in
September 1939 had left the "reunited" National Party. Many
of these entered the 1943 elections against Malan, throwing

[8]By implication a new category is also needed to describe the 1948
election, for if it was not a "realigning" election, it certainly was
not a "maintaining," "deviating," or "reinstating" election. Alter-
natively, and it would be my preference, the requirement that a
"realigning" election must show a *sharp* as well as a durable
realignment in the partisan attachments of the electorate might
be relaxed. A solution to this problem fortunately is not required
here, but the problem itself highlights the difficulty of using a
typology of elections that combines two variables — election outcome and degree of voter realignment — in the context of a party
system that has become closely balanced.

at least four seats to Smuts. A second factor was the continued opposition of the Nationalists to South African participation in the war against Germany. Advocacy of neutrality in 1939 was one thing; to wish to sue for peace in 1943 was no doubt seen by many voters as something different. A third electoral liability was the commitment of the National Party in 1942 to the transformation of South Africa into an authoritarian republic outside the British Commonwealth, a republic wherein Afrikaner values would be clearly dominant. This was openly reactionary. Finally, there was the fact of South Africa's involvement in a war whose course had improved by the middle of 1943 from the standpoint of the Allies. The electorate could be expected to be reluctant to turn out the government in the midst of the country's prosecution of a war, all the more so at a time when the war effort appeared to be at last successful. From the standpoint of the process of national integration, the interrelated first and third items listed above are of particular interest, and accordingly we shall treat them in some detail below.[9]

In their article on the integrative process that has been cited above, Philip Jacob and Henry Teune identify the importance of previous integrative experience. Successful efforts at integration have, they suggest, a "spill-over" effect, making it possible for future integration to occur more easily. "But," they caution, "the reinforcement principle is symmetrical. Integrative experiences, in order to contribute to a generalized habit of integration, must be rewarded. If they are not rewarded or are punished they may encourage habits which lead to disintegration."[10] In the last chapter I have suggested that the end of Fusion in 1939 did more than allow for the reconciliation of those Afrikaners in the electorate

[9]The account of political cross-currents within Afrikanerdom during World War II that is provided by Roberts and Trollip in their book, *The South African Opposition, 1939-1945,* is impressively thorough. Accordingly, this chapter provides only the minimum summary that is necessary for its purposes. The continuation of this story into the postwar years that is found in Chapters VII and VIII is less "bare bones," recognizing that it is not available in as great detail elsewhere.

[10]Jacob and Teune, "The Integrative Process," p. 44.

who had divided in 1934; it discredited the doctrine of "conciliation" which had made Fusion possible. Afrikaners generalized from the experience of 1939: the English-speaking community not only had not stood by the principle of "South Africa first," its members could not. After 1939 most of those Afrikaners who had followed Hertzog into the United Party appear to have come to believe with Malan that the only nationalism in South Africa worthy of the name was Afrikaner nationalism, and the clearest expression of this belief became republicanism.

A particular appeal of republicanism for Afrikaners in the early 1940s was the finality the coming of a republic would give to all the constitutional questions that had plagued the Union since its inception. On January 27, 1940, terms of a Hereniging (conciliation) agreement that had been signed by both Hertzog and Malan were published in the press. The agreement stated that the parliamentary caucuses of the "purified" National Party and the Hertzog "Group" had agreed to consolidate as a single party, to be known as the Reunited National Party or People's Party (die Herenigde Nasionale, of Volksparty), the HNP. Until such time as a statement of principles could be drawn up, the agreement continued, "best use" would be made of the existing "programmes" of both groups. However, the following statement on the republican issue, with emphasis added, was accepted:

The party unreservedly acknowledges the right of the people, whenever it is regarded as being in the interest of the country, to change the form of government along constitutional lines. The party is convinced that the republican form of government, separated from the British Crown, will be best suited to the traditions, circumstances and aspirations of the South African nation, *and is the only effective guarantee that South Africa will not again be drawn into the wars of Great Britain.*

The party will therefore endeavor to remove all irregularities that might obstruct the realization of the national freedom.

The party acknowledges that a republic can be achieved only on the broad basis of the nation's will and with full regard to the equal language and cultural rights of the two sections of the European population. In accordance with this principle it is provided that this constitutional change can be brought about only in terms of a special and definite mandate from the majority of the European voters and not merely as the result of a parliamentary majority that may be obtained at a general election. Membership of the party will not be denied or refused to any national-minded Afrikaner who is prepared to subject himself to the party obligations, but who is not convinced of the desirability of establishing a republic in the existing circumstances.[11]

The last sentence of this statement, curiously different in tone from the first paragraph, was the price of the support of Hertzog, who now became the leader of the HNP in Parliament. During the discussions between Hertzog and the "purified" Nationalists on the formation of the new party, disagreement had been encountered on the question of the future party's commitment to the creation of a republic, among other matters. Hertzog believed that while very many Afrikaners recognized the republic as an ideal, there were others who did not, and the new party ought to include Afrikaners of both schools of thought who were united in their opposition to Smuts. What Hertzog wanted, therefore, was acceptance of the position on the republican question that the old National Party had, at Hertzog's insistence, adopted in 1927, namely, that while allowing freedom of individual expression on the matter, the party itself accepted the resolution of the Imperial Conference of 1926 regarding the sovereignty and independence of the dominions.[12] But the "purified" Nationalists had moved a considerable distance away from the position adopted in 1927 during the intervening years, and mere permission to make republican propaganda was no longer, if indeed it ever had been, sufficient for such as Strijdom. In the end, the leaders could scarcely stand

[11]*The Star,* January 29, 1940.
[12]Change in the National Party's *Programme of Principles,* Article 4, made in 1927. Quoted by Kruger (ed.), *South African Parties and Policies,* p. 70n.

against a popular wish for the creation of a politically united Afrikanerdom, or forego its considerable promise of electoral support. They papered over their differences or agreed to postpone their resolution. Hereniging was accordingly achieved, at least in form, and a new political entity was created that seemed likely in time to gain the support of most of those electors who had supported the National Party only a decade earlier.

But this unity was short-lived. Predictably, the question of the HNP's commitment to the creation of a republic soon reemerged and separated "reunited" Nationalists. Even those who could agree that a republic ought to be an object of HNP policy fell out as to how a republic might be best achieved, and what the nature of a future republic should be. At the beginning of 1942, just under two years after the signing of the Hereniging agreement, "reunited" Afrikanerdom was again divided, this time among the HNP and three other political entities, each with its distinctive point of view.

The Afrikaner Party

The first break can be dated November 6, 1940. The occasion was the first congress of the HNP meeting in Bloemfontein, and the issue was the adoption of a "programme of principles" for the HNP in the Free State. Two statements were placed before the congress. One had been prepared by the Federal Council of the HNP; the other had been prepared by Hertzog. There were a number of differences. In contrast with Hertzog's draft, that of the Federal Council spoke of the development and application of a republican constitution as soon as possible and the recognition of "Die Stem" as South Africa's only national anthem. Most important to Hertzog was the failure of the Federal Council's draft to make any reference to equality of status and political rights for English-speaking whites. No doubt was left in the minds of the delegates that Hertzog would view rejection of his draft as a vote of no-confidence in his leadership, and soon after the congress did in fact reject it by an overwhelming majority, Hertzog rose and dramatically announced his resignation of the leadership of the Free State HNP. Followed by approximately one hundred others, Hertzog then left the congress. C. R. Swart, who was subsequently elected to Hertzog's place as leader of the party in the Free State, spoke of his regret that Hertzog had seen fit to resign on what amounted to "the rights of the English-speaking people."[13]

On December 12, nine days after a meeting of the Transvaal congress of the HNP that prohibited any discussion of the "Bloemfontein happenings," Hertzog, responding to what he termed a "lack of trust" in both the Free State and the Transvaal, resigned his seat in the House of Assembly. "The party," Hertzog declared in a letter to his constituents, "is following a course which . . . must necessarily lead to the downfall of Afrikanerdom."[14] Hertzog's longtime associates, N. C. Havenga and Senator J. Brebner, resigned their parliamentary seats with him. Thus six weeks later when E. A. Conroy announced in the House of Assembly the founding of the Afrikaner Party, the AP, as a political home for Hertzogites, Hertzog himself and two of his foremost lieutenants had already retired from public life. This unnecessarily burdened the new party, for "Hertzogism" (as the doctrine of equal rights for both language groups was sometimes called) without Hertzog proved to have lost much of its former popular appeal.

The political marriage that had been Hereniging was now clearly over, although the HNP continued to insist the opposite was true. But had it ended, to continue the metaphor, through divorce or the death of one of the partners? The issue was of the greatest importance in the matter of the liquidation of the electoral estate. An answer to this question was not immediately forthcoming, but such evidence as was available suggested that despite the creation of the Afrikaner Party, Hertzogism had died politically. Of the 38 United Party MP's who had voted against war on September 4, 1939, only ten joined the Afrikaner Party. None had had previous ministerial experience, and few could be said to have been

[13]*The Friend,* October 29, 30; November 7, 1940.
[14]*The Friend,* December 13, 1940. This letter was also signed by N. C. Havenga.

politically prominent. The Smithfield and Fauresmith by-elections of March 1941, necessitated by the resignations of Hertzog and Havenga, provided the first electoral test of the Afrikaner Party, for the United Party left it to the AP to oppose the HNP in each constituency. The new party could have hoped to find no more favorable battle conditions, yet in each case its candidate was humiliated, neither receiving more than 44 percent of the vote. Time might allow for improvement in the electoral organization of the Afrikaner Party, but for the moment it could be considered only a parliamentary caucus with a life expectancy no greater than the House itself.

The New Order

The loyal adherents of Hertzogism had scarcely been driven from the HNP when its triumphant leadership was again faced with a threat to its authority in the matter of party doctrine. The issue was no longer the "rights of the English" or the republican credo, but parliamentary democracy itself.

Sigmund Neumann has suggested that the further a party is from power, the more likely it is that it will shun day-by-day "expediency interests" in favor of "the fundamental principles of an all-inclusive 'faith movement.' "[15] And in a similar vein, Franz Neumann has hypothesized that loss of status on the part of a group, especially when that loss is poorly understood, generally leads to political alienation, that is, the conscious rejection of the "rules of the game" of the political system.[16] Together these propositions suggest a partial explanation for the emergence in 1941 of an organized pressure group within the parliamentary caucus of the HNP identifying with the ideology of National-Socialism, and calling itself the New Order Group.

The leader of this body was Oswald Pirow, former Minister of Defense in the last Hertzog government who even in office

[15]Sigmund Neumann, "Toward a Comparative Study of Political Parties," in Sigmund Neumann (ed.), *Modern Political Parties: Approaches to Comparative Politics* (Chicago: University of Chicago Press, 1956), p. 400.
[16]Franz Neumann, *The Democratic and the Authoritarian State,* (Glencoe: The Free Press, 1957), p. 293.

had exhibited admiration for Germany's Nazi leaders. Its members included a majority of the Hertzogite MP's who had not left the HNP for the Afrikaner Party. For these men, it was possible that September 4, 1939, marked the apex of their political careers, for did not both Smuts and the former leadership of the "purified" National Party now stand between them and cabinet office? In the 1930's, for example, Pirow had been spoken of as a future prime minister, but now Malan, Strijdom, and Swart would seem to have moved into line ahead of him. Moreover, for his part it is clear that Pirow viewed the decision of September 4 as the product of a dark conspiracy — in the words of F.S. Crafford that Pirow quotes approvingly, the plucked fruit of "years of planning, concession, and compromise: the subversion of neutrality at the eleventh hour. . . . It was a masterpiece of strategy."[17] The result of these beliefs was the organization of a "faith movement" preaching the end of "liberal-capitalist-democracy." What would follow in the Union, according to Pirow, would be a "New Order" that, under God's guidance, would sweep away democracy and substitute a Christian, white, National-Socialist republic, separated from the British Crown and founded on the principles of state authority ("Staatsgesag") and national discipline. In December 1940, these ideas were published in a pamphlet entitled (in Afrikaans) *New Order for South Africa* by a body calling itself the Christian Republican South African National-Socialist Study Circle, later known simply as the New Order. By the middle of 1941 this pamphlet had been through seven editions, and the New Order had a Pretoria postal address and a national organizer.

The Malanite leadership of the HNP could scarcely welcome Pirow's public declarations that Parliament (as it was then constituted), elections, and "party politics" were outdated and unnecessary, for the electorate might conclude that even the HNP in its existing form was an effete organization. The continued propagation of National-Socialism within the HNP, and public espousal of it by some members, could only divide the party's membership, blur the definition of its policy,

[17] Pirow, *James Barry Munnik Hertzog,* p. 245.

and drive its supporters into other channels of political expression, thus weakening the party's electoral standing. Malan and the other established leaders of the HNP therefore looked forward to the day when the New Orderites might be brought to heel, and throughout 1941 they waged an unremitting campaign against "group formation" within the party. The climax of this campaign arrived on January 14, 1942, when, in a letter to Malan, Pirow announced that the New Orderites would not attend the HNP caucus but would function as an independent parliamentary group.[18] Pirow incongruously asserted that the New Orderites would remain within the party, but this did not disguise the fact that within a year the HNP had split a second time at the parliamentary level. Of the 38 United Party MP's who had crossed into opposition on September 4, 1939, only nine were to be found in the HNP after January 14, 1942. Of the remainder, three had resigned from Parliament, ten had joined the Afrikaner Party and sixteen were in the New Order.

The Ossewa-Brandwag

In the same year that saw the founding of the Afrikaner Party and the emergence of the independent-minded New Order within the HNP, yet another challenge emerged to the claim of the Malanite leadership of the HNP that it alone spoke for "national-minded" Afrikanerdom, this time from a source outside the framework of the parliamentary system, namely, the Ossewa-Brandwag (Ox Wagon Sentinel), or OB. In the course of 1941, the OB threatened not only to usurp the role of the HNP, but, in leading a growing number of Afrikaners into extra-parliamentary and even extra-constitutional avenues of political expression, perhaps to obviate that role in the minds of its followers. The founding of the OB as a paramilitary Afrikaner nationalist cultural organization occurred at the time of the 1938 Voortrekker Centenary celebrations; and in a vivid illustration of the Franz Neumann's hypothesis that groups losing status are likely to reject the "rules of the game," the decision of September 4, 1939, gave fresh impetus to the movement, and thereafter

[18]*Rand Daily Mail,* January 15, 1942.

it spread quickly. Hans van Rensburg, who became commandant-general of the organization in January 1941, writes,
"Men were keyed up. They were looking for activist ranks."[19]
These ranks the OB provided. It also appeared to provide
a means of self-defense against the social and economic
pressures to which antiwar-Afrikaners were commonly subjected.

The constituent element of the OB was the "commando,"
a unit approximately the size of a military company, comprised of persons who lived in the same town, or in the same
neighborhood of a large town. Initially, both men and women
might belong; later only men could become members. The
OB had an informal uniform patterned on the attire worn
by the Voortrekkers, a flag, a salute, and a badge, the latter
bearing some resemblance to the badge of the German National-Socialists of the period. OB officers were elected at each
level of the organization's hierarchial structure. Commandoes,
and the "sections" into which they were sub-divided, drilled,
held parades, had discussions on cultural and historical topics,
appeared on certain Afrikaner public occasions, and organized
outings of a sporting and cultural nature. The organization
focused upon Afrikaner cultural and Afrikaner community
activity and its spirit was undeniably martial. In its paraphernalia, organization, activities, and manner, the OB resembled
both the Voortrekker Movement (the Afrikaner equivalent
after 1931 of the South African Scouting Movement) and
a somewhat informal civilian army. After the outbreak of
World War II, the OB's resemblance to the latter increased.
On February 4, 1941, Malan told the House of Assembly that
the OB had between 300,000 and 400,000 members.[20]

The emergence of an active organization of "national-
minded" Afrikaners of such size could not but be welcomed
by Malan provided that that organization limited itself to
the achievement of its avowed non-political ends and did not
encroach upon the political prerogatives of the HNP. On

[20]*House of Assembly Debates,* Vol. 41, 1940-41, col. 2195.
[19]Hans van Rensburg, *Their Paths Crossed Mine: Memoirs of the
Commandant-General of the Ossewa-Brandwag* (South Africa:
Central News Agency, 1956), p. 159.

October 29, 1940, Malan had discussions with the OB executive on this point in Bloemfontein, and the next day at
Cradock in the Cape Province he announced the terms of
an agreement with the OB. It was essentially a simple
statement: "The assurance exists that neither . . . [body]
will interfere or meddle with the affairs or in the domain
of the other."[21] Yet less than three months later the leaders
of the two organizations were hopelessly at odds, for in
practice the domain of the party, as understood by its
leadership, overlapped that of the OB, as viewed by its
executive. Malan claimed for the party the exclusive right
to decide all political questions on behalf of "national-minded" Afrikanerdom, but van Rensburg would concede the HNP
only the narrower field termed "party-politics," an imprecise
conception approximately meaning the scope and workings
of the parliamentary system. Gradually, the OB came to
reflect a distinctive political outlook and program, one that
was fundamentally incompatible with the essentially democratic — certainly, at least, parliamentary — program and
outlook of the party.

The beginning of the end of cooperation between the two
bodies is possibly best dated July 3, 1941. On that date, the
OB distributed widely (100,000 copies) a circular letter, *Uniale
Omsendbrief 1/41,* containing details of a proposed republican
constitution. In circulating this document, the OB had made
an unmistakable and unforgivable encroachment upon the
political rights of the party. Thereafter the HNP leadership
worked earnestly to bring the OB under the control of the
party, and when that effort failed, to destroy it. On October
3, 1941, Malan called on all members of the HNP to resign
from the OB,[22] and thereafter OB resignation lists appeared
nearly daily in the pages of *Die Transvaler, Die Volksblad,*
and *Die Burger.* A week later, on Kruger Day, the party
launched an offensive in the Transvaal where the OB, with
an estimated membership of 130,000, was a formidable force.
As elsewhere in the country at the same time, all the resources

[21] *The Friend,* October 31, 1940.
[22] *The Star,* October 3, 1941.

of the HNP were brought into a concerted attack on van Rensburg, his organization, and the National-Socialism to which, it was now said, that organization gave whole-hearted support. These were, however, but the opening shots between the HNP and the OB in a political war that was to last for several years before the ultimate victory of the party was assured.

Meanwhile, the dispute between Malan and van Rensburg in the second half of 1941 appears to have resulted in some public doubt being cast on the willingness of the HNP leadership not only to consider, but to prepare in detail for, the realization of its expressed republican ideal, doubt van Rensburg clearly hoped to increase. To reestablish his standing as a republican, and possibly to reunite his evidently divided caucus (the New Orderites announced their withdrawal from the caucus the next day), Malan moved the establishment of a "free and independent" republic in South Africa in the House of Assembly on January 13, 1942.[23] And ten days later, *Die Transvaler* and *Die Burger* published, with Malan's express permission, a detailed draft republican constitution that the two papers said could be taken "as an indication of the general direction which the Party has already adopted."[24] One reason Malan had decided to release the constitution, the papers indicated, was the "unauthorized use which has formerly been made of portion of it," a reference to the OB's *Uniale Omsendbrief 1/41*. A comparison between the two documents shows the first-published to have been a summary of the second. At the beginning of this chapter, I described this draft constitution as authoritarian and reactionary. The following passages from the constitution may suffice to justify this description:

The National Flag is the Vierkleur of the Old South African Republic, with the red band replaced by one of

[23]*House of Assembly Debates,* Vol. 43, 1942, cols. 33-34.
[24]The constitution has been reproduced in English translation in two places: *British Africa Monthly,* July 1948; and International Commission of Jurists, *South Africa and the Rule of Law* (Geneva, 1960), Appendix B.

orange; the National Anthem of the Republic will be "Die Stem van Suid-Afrika."

Afrikaans . . . will be the first official language. English will be regarded as a second or supplemental official language which will be treated on an equal footing . . . whenever such treatment is judged by the State authority to be in the best interest of the State. . . .

All people . . . within the bounds of the Republic are its subjects and subject to its authority. . . . The white subjects . . . will be called "burgers". . . . Only "Burgers" can obtain the right to vote. . . .

The State President is chosen by the registered burgers. . . . [He is] only responsible to God . . . for his deeds in the fulfillment of his duties. . . .

In time of National danger the State President [can] suspend . . . this Constitution. . . .

The constituencies will be divided every five years by a judicial commission. . . . It may fix the number of electors in a [rural] constituency at under 20 percent and in urban constituencies up to 20 percent over the quota fixed by legislation. . . .

A Community Council, . . . with exclusively advisory powers, will be constituted. . . . The members consist of . . . persons appointed . . . on account of their knowledge and experience in connection with the treatment of important problems of the country, [such as] the Indian penetration, and the surplus Jewish population . . .

Every Coloured group of Races, Coloured, Natives, Asiatics, Indians, etc., will be segregated, not only as regards the place of dwelling or the neighborhoods dwelt in by them but also with regard to spheres of work.

White employees may not be employed by non-European employers.

The public tone of life of the Republic is Christian-National. . . . The propagation of any state policy and the existence of any political organization which is in strife with the fulfilling of this Christian-National vocation of the life of the people is forbidden.

William H. Vatcher reports that "English-speaking South Africans were shocked by the Draft Constitution," and it seems likely that many Afrikaner moderates were as well.[25] It was never considered or approved by any congress of the HNP.

The 1943 Elections

Early in 1943, with a general election widely expected no later than August, van Rensburg addressed identical letters to Malan, Pirow and Havenga, the latter having become the leader of the Afrikaner Party. After some preliminary remarks designed to show how uninterested the OB was in elections generally, and in the next election in particular, which, it was said, could not result in a change in government, van Rensburg offered an election pact: "In each constituency in which the party organizations of Afrikanerdom agree to put forward a mutually acceptable Volk candidate, such candidate will be assured not only of the votes but also of the organizational support of the Ossewa-Brandwag."[26]

To become effective, van Rensburg's offer had to be accepted by Pirow, Havenga, *and* Malan. The first two consented to the arrangement, but Malan ignored the offer, subsequently repeated, except to require all aspirant HNP candidates to declare that they were members of no other party or movement.[27] Thus rebuffed, the OB ceased to concern itself officially with the forthcoming election.

The New Order was the next to leave the electoral field. On March 30, 1943, the New Order caucus issued the following statement:

Taking cognizance of the fact that the present unfortu-

[25]William Henry Vatcher, Jr., *White Laager: The Rise of Afrikaner Nationalism* (New York: Frederick A. Praeger, 1965), p. 73.
[26]Information Service of the O.B., *Die Ossewa-Brandwag en I. die Parlementsverkiesing; II. die Soldate; III. die Kommunisme* (O.B. Uitgawe Nr. 3; Johannesburg, April 1943), p. 9.
[27]A. J. H. van der Walt, *'n Volk op Trek of 'n Kort Geskiedenis van die Ontstaan en Ontwikkeling van die Ossewabrandwag* (O.B. Uitgawe nr. 5; Johannesburg: Handelsreklamediens Bpk., 1944), p. 118.

nate division among Nationalist-minded Afrikaners is being aggravated by competition for Parliamentary ... seats in connection with the forthcoming elections, and as a genuine contribution to ultimate effective national-unity on the basis of Afrikaner National-Socialism, the chief study circle and caucus of the New Order decided:

(1) That no member of the New Order shall offer himself as an independent, or in any other capacity, as a candidate for election to the House of Assembly ... in connection with the forthcoming elections.

(2) That, in the forthcoming elections, the New Order will exert all its strength unconditionally against General Smuts and Communism.[28]

Faced with the prospect that, unallied, three-quarters or more of its MP's would be defeated in the coming election, the New Order seemed to choose voluntary exile from Parliament rather than the stigma of public rejection.

The Afrikaner Party now sought an electoral alliance with the HNP, and in the middle of April discussions took place between Malan and Havenga in Cape Town. Havenga asked that Malan support the AP in the eight constituencies then held by the party. In turn, the AP would support HNP candidates elsewhere, but Havenga would not commit his party to cooperate with Malan after the election. Thus for his conceding a half-dozen or so likely HNP victories to the AP, Malan was to receive only the questionable and, in any case, perhaps unnecessary support of the Afrikaner Party in other seats until such time as the election was held. Not surprisingly, Malan turned down this offer as a bad bargain, and the two parties entered upon the subsequent campaign unallied.[29]

On May 15, 1943, Prime Minister Smuts announced that the general election would be held on July 7. The House of Assembly was dissolved on May 29, at which time its composition was as follows:

---

[28]*The Friend,* March 31, 1943.
[29]Roberts and Trollip, *The South African Opposition,* p. 148.

Government Coalition (86 seats)

United Party	71
Dominion Party	8
Labour Party	4
Natives Representatives[30]	3

Opposition (65 seats)

HNP	40
AP	8
New Order	16
Independent	1

Nomination day was June 14, at the close of which 334 candidates had been nominated in the 150 constituencies; 18 of these were nominated unopposed and declared forthwith elected, including only Malan for Picketberg among opposition candidates. The HNP nominated 110 candidates, and the Afrikaner Party 24. Also nominated were 12 so-called Volkseenheid (Volk-unity) candidates and 1 Independent Republican, all in the Transvaal. More than half the number of HNP candidates in the Transvaal stood in urban seats, 23 on the Witwatersrand and 8 in Pretoria.

The 12 Volkseenheid candidates in the Transvaal require some identification. No alliance amongst them was evident, although they did appear to represent in common a desire for the achievement of a united front of "national-minded" Afrikaners outside the HNP, and they did receive some support from the Afrikaner Party, the OB, and the New Order. One of the 12 was a New Order MP who defied its ban on standing for reelection, and a second was prominent in the OB. Five of the 12 withdrew from the election before July 7 under pressure from the HNP, although their names remained on the ballot and drew some votes. Indeed, in one instance the retired Volkseenheid candidate received more

[30]The three Natives' Representatives were unaffected by the dissolution as their seats were filled at fixed intervals.

votes than the majority of the victorious candidate of the United Party.

Until Smuts' announcement on May 15, it was widely believed that the general election would occur in August. Malan complained, therefore, that Smuts had called a "snap" election, but in fact all parties had been campaigning since early in the year — the campaign of the HNP had really begun with the party's Union congress in Pretoria in September 1942. However, the HNP election manifesto was not issued until June 15. In it, prime consideration was given not to attacking the government, but to the challenge of other opposition groups, termed "the wreckers of Afrikanerdom." Subsequent points dealt with the desirability of a republic, the need for maintaining "white civilization," and a guarantee of equal political, language, and cultural rights for English-speaking South Africans.[31] This last point attempted to counter the charge of both the Afrikaner Party and the government that the HNP was interested only in the rights of Afrikaners. (In fact, the HNP manifesto was remarkably similar to the election statement of the Afrikaner Party in all but a few minor respects.)

Although HNP's campaign appeal spoke of several matters, under the circumstances the campaign was necessarily a single-issue affair, that issue being the Union's continued participation in the war. The course of the war, that two or three years earlier had drawn support to the opposition's antiwar policy, now seemed to favor the government. By election day the Germans and Italians had been swept from North Africa with the assistance of South African forces, and the German advance into Russia had been stopped short of Moscow and reversed. An Allied invasion of Europe clearly lay ahead. Though Malan had complained earlier of military parades being held during the campaign, Smuts apparently felt no political liability in appearing at a military review at Turffontein on June 26 and calling for volunteers for service "beyond Africa."[32]

Indeed, after the entry of Japan on the side of the Axis

[31] *The Friend,* June 21, 1943.
[32] *The Friend,* June 28, 1943.

on December 7, 1941, an increasing number of Afrikaner moderates who had supported Hertzog in September 1939 came to believe that continued opposition to the war was politically irresponsible. Early in 1942, for example, A. C. Cilliers, a well-known academic figure and now chief propagandist for the Afrikaner Party, wrote: "Our heritage is in danger! A crafty enemy lies in wait before the portals of our land! Awake, stand up, and prepare yourself for the defense of nation and fatherland." And, "The Afrikaner who is not frightened of a victory of Hitler and the Axis is blind, stupid, or himself a Nazi in inclination."[33] On March 30, 1942, the *Cape Argus* reported that the head committee of the Afrikaner Party in the Transvaal, following the lead of its counterpart in the Free State, and after declaring that "the Afrikaner . . . is not blind to international developments," had resolved not to do anything that might "hamper" the government's war policy. But with the coming of this attitude, some members of the Afrikaner Party took the next step and rejoined the United Party. Among these, by the beginning of the 1943 parliamentary session, were two MP's and two senators. And even though Havenga called on the voters to reject the government's war policy, the Afrikaner Party's election manifesto in 1943 came out against South Africa's concluding a separate and independent peace.

By election day even Malan was equivocating on the war issue. Speaking at Pretoria on May 24, the Volksleier (Volkleader), as Malan was now called by his partisans, said that if the HNP were returned to power, he would bring the South African troops back to the Union where they would defend its borders. But whether or not peace would be made with Germany "would depend on circumstances," Malan said.[34] And at Caledon on June 16, Malan claimed that "even if the decision to go to war had been right," South Africans had already "done their share."[35] The HNP even made an effort to win the votes of the 149,000 men and women in

[33]A. C. Cilliers, *Afrikaners Ontwaak* (Stellenbosch: Pro Ecclesia-Drukkery, [1942]), pp. 25,32.
[34]*The Friend,* May 25, 1943.
[35]*The Friend,* June 17, 1943.

uniform who had been especially registered for the election. Some 70 percent of South African troops were Afrikaans-speaking, but all were volunteers, although certainly not all for reason of their support of the government's war policy.[36] Tactfully ignoring a considerable past record to the contrary, Malan claimed that the HNP had "always honoured the soldier, whatever his political convictions may be, who offers his life for his country."[37] The party also promised to "respect and execute all existing obligations in connection with soldier's grants and pensions, with the exception of those which the Smuts government has awarded to non-white soldiers."[38]

Although election day was July 7, the transmission, sorting, and counting of the soldiers' votes delayed the announcement of the results until the last week of the month when it appeared that Smuts had achieved an astonishing triumph. Government coalition candidates had succeeded in 65 of 68 urban seats and in 42 of 82 rural seats. The United Party had a majority in the House of Assembly of 28; with the other parties to the coalition, a majority of 64 was possible. The antiwar coalition had lost a total of 23 seats. J. L. Grey calculated that 63.9 percent of the entire voting electorate would have voted "for war" had there been election contests in every constituency. On the same basis, Grey estimated that 31.9 percent of the Afrikaans-speaking electorate supported Smuts.[39] When taken with the comparable figure for the 1938 general election (40.4 percent), the statistic suggests that only one of every four Afrikaners who had voted for the United Party in 1938 voted against Smuts in 1943. From Malan's viewpoint, this was a small dividend for the break-up of Fusion in 1939.

Yet there was another side to the 1943 election results. First, although none of the rival opposition candidates was successful, their appearance seems to have thrown the election from the HNP to the United Party in four instances, all

---

[36]Leo Marguard, *The Peoples and Policies of South Africa* (London: Oxford University Press, 1952), p. 208.
[37]*The Friend,* June 19, 1943.
[38]HNP campaign literature.
[39]J. L. Gray, "How the Nation Voted."

1943 Election Results

United Party	89	HNP	43
Labour Party	9	Afrikaner Party	0
Dominion Party	7	Independents (pro-war)	2

in the Transvaal. Second, it seems clear that thousands of Afrikaners abstained from voting in 1943 as a deliberate political act. Michael Roberts and A.E.G. Trollip are wrong when they state that the "total poll was some 300,000 less than in 1938, not counting uncontested seats."[40] Actually, 50,000 *more* votes were cast in 1943 than in 1939, but the percentage poll in contested seats, 75.3 percent, was smaller than in either 1938 or 1948. Moreover, in seats lost by the opposition, the turnout was particularly low, 303 votes lower on the average than in seats the opposition won. Several by-elections held soon after the 1943 general election showed a larger total vote than at the general election *and* an increase in the total vote for the HNP candidate that was considerably greater than the reduction in the United Party vote. Such results could be explained as a return to the polls of opposition supporters who had abstained in 1943. An added 303 votes would have given Malan only a half-dozen extra seats in 1943. However, it would have placed an HNP victory within only 500 votes in 16 constituencies, and within 1,000 votes in 25 of them.

A third conclusion was that the anti-Smuts forces had lost electoral support to the government *after* the war vote of September 1939. Although a redrawing of constituency boundaries in 1943 makes an exact comparison of constituency returns both before and after this redrawing impossible, it seems noteworthy nevertheless that in every one of five constituencies where there had been a by-election since the beginning of the war, government support was up in 1943. This suggests the importance of the immediate circumstances of the election, circumstances that Roberts and Trollip agree were "exceptionally unfavorable" from the standpoint of the opposition.[41]

[40]Roberts and Trollip, *The South African Opposition,* p. 160.
[41]*Ibid.*, p. 159.

Fourth, the government's victories had come largely at the expense of the Afrikaner Party and the New Order, both of which were now eliminated from Parliament. On Malan's hard core support, Smuts had made few inroads. The HNP lost only 8 seats, all to the United Party, while concurrently winning 2 seats from Smuts, 5 from the Afrikaner Party, and 6 from the New Order. When the HNP parliamentary caucus reassembled in Cape Town, it was actually larger by 3. In particular, the 1943 elections humiliated the Afrikaner Party. Only 2 of its 23 candidates managed to poll more than 1,000 votes, the best performance being that of Havenga who received 1,487 votes at Frankfurt in the Free State. Commenting on the election, Havenga acknowledged that "conciliation" was a dead issue, a casuality of the war. "The Nationalism of General Hertzog," he said, "based on absolute equality and unity of the people, has been rejected. We cannot but regret it, but it would be futile for us not to face the fact."[42] Meanwhile, Malan observed that the "one satisfactory aspect of this election" was that "the Opposition is once again one consolidated whole."[43] The HNP was now thus the only possible alternative government. But more than this, it was, in the words of Roberts and Trollip, "a very *probable* alternative Government in the not too distant future."[44]

Finally, even though only one of 23 HNP candidates on the Witwatersrand was successful, the fact that these candidates received 31.9 percent of the total vote was grounds for Malan being optimistic, for in 1938 the "purified" National Party had fought 16 seats on the Witwatersrand and received only 23.6 percent of the vote. The HNP expended particular energy on the Witwatersrand in 1943, concentrating on seats where it was hoped the previous efforts of "nation-minded" trade union "reformers," among other considerations, might pay electoral dividends. Well might the HNP continue this effort. After the general election of 1943, the HNP controlled 43 seats in the House of Assembly and had little prospect of a political alliance with any other party represented in

[42]*Rand Daily Mail,* July 30, 1943, copying *Die Vaderland.*
[43]*The Friend,* July 31, 1943.
[44]Roberts and Trollip, *The South African Opposition,* p. 160.

the House. Malan thus lacked 34 of the minimum of 77 seats he needed if he were to come to power unassisted. The results of the 1943 election suggested that if the party were to obtain 34 additional seats, 11 would probably come from the Cape, Natal would probably produce 2, and 21 would be from the Transvaal. (See Figure 1.) And of the 21 Transvaal seats seemingly most within the grasp of the HNP, 5 were seats on the Witwatersrand. Indeed, in each of 5 Witwatersrand contests in 1943, the HNP candidate was defeated by fewer than 840 votes.

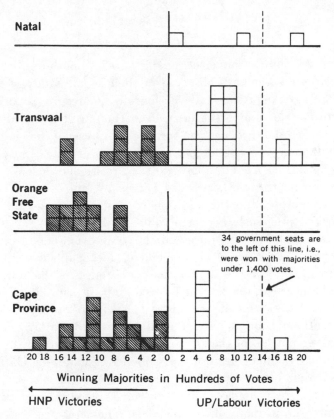

Figure 1. The 1943 General Election. Seats won and lost by the HNP by less than 2,000 votes. (Each square represents one constituency.)

6.

Some Demographic Changes

As Philip Converse and his three co-authors of *The American Voter* have observed in their sequel study of the 1960 American presidential election, election results can differ from one election to the next, even though no voter alters his earlier political choice, because of physical changes or spatial changes in the composition of the electorate.[1] Physical change arises from the involuntary retirement each year through death or otherwise of between 1 and 2 percent of the electorate, and the addition to the rolls of new voters who had previously been ineligible, usually because of age. Spatial change is the movement of voters from one election district to another. Such movement does not show up in national vote totals if the political preferences of the individuals concerned remain unchanged, but it can affect the electoral decisions at the district level. In South Africa, generational changes have gradually increased the Afrikaans-speaking portion of the electorate, while white urbanization has had two direct electoral consequences. First, it has shifted political influence from the rural areas to the cities, and second, it has increased the Afrikaans-speaking proportion of the vote in many urban districts. The vital processes of the electorate have clearly favored the National Party, and on balance it would appear that white urbanization has done so as well.

[1]Philip E. Converse *et al.*, "Stability and Change in 1960," p. 271.

Throughout the present century, the white population of South Africa has increased at a rate that has varied between 1.7 percent and 2.2 percent per annum.[2] Among Afrikaners, however, the rate of annual natural increase has been greater than this. On April 26, 1943, an editorial in *Die Transvaler* cited 1936 Union census figures to show that at the time that census was taken: (1) for every 100 English-speaking persons over 21 years of age, there were 115 Afrikaans-speaking persons; (2) for every 100 English-speaking persons between the ages of 7 and 21 years, there were 185 Afrikaans-speaking persons; and (3) for every 100 English-speaking persons under 7 years of age, there were 212 Afrikaans-speaking persons. This editorial was entitled "Have Confidence in the Future." Well might "reunited" Nationalists take comfort from the fact that the Afrikaans-speaking section of the white population, which even in 1938 had given a majority of its votes to the "purified" National Party, was undergoing a rate of natural increase that was markedly faster than that of the English-speaking section.

The Union census of 1946 confirmed the fact of a more rapid rate of natural increase among Afrikaners. Over the decade separating the two population counts, the percentage of whites speaking Afrikaans as the home language rose from 55.9 percent to 57.3 percent. During the same period, the percentage of whites over 21 years of age (and thus eligible for the vote) speaking Afrikaans as the home language rose from 53.5 percent to 54.4 percent.[3] Extrapolating from these figures, it seems that between 1943 and 1948, the percentage of Afrikaners in the electorate probably increased an average of 0.1 percent annually, or by 45 votes in every 9,000 (the average number of voters per constituency in 1948) over the full five-year period. This would not appear to have been enough to have made the rate of natural increase among Afrikaners an important factor in the 1948 election, but

[2]*Official Year Book,* No. 29, 1956-1957, p. 712.
[3]Union of South Africa, *Sixth Census of the Population of the Union of South Africa* (enumerated 5th May, 1936), U.G. No. 44, for 1938, Vol. IV, Table No. 7, p. 66; Union of South Africa, *Census of the Population of the Union of South Africa* (enumerated 7th May 1946) U.G. No. 18 for 1954, Vol. IV, Table No. 15, p. 78.

obviously its significance over a longer period of time would be appreciable.

Still another conclusion that could be drawn from the 1946 Union census figures was that the rural exodus of whites to the cities, which had begun even before 1910, continued. The growth of the percentage of the white population that was located within the country's urban areas demonstrates the speed of white urbanization over two and one-half decades: the percentage was 55.8 in 1921, 58.2 in 1926, 61.3 in 1931, and 65.2 in 1936; by 1946, it was 72.5.[4]

This growth in the proportion of whites living in urban centers between 1936 and 1946 necessarily resulted in successive delimitation commissions awarding a larger number of parliamentary seats to these areas at the expense of the rural districts. The Seventh Delimitation Commission in 1937 gave 59 seats to the urban areas. The Eighth increased this number to 68 in 1943, and the Ninth added two more in 1948. The Witwatersrand region was the principal beneficiary of these redelimitations. In 1943 the number of Rand constituencies was increased from 26 to 32, and in 1948 the number grew to 34. In 1943 the nine new urban seats were made available by eliminating three constituencies in the rural Transvaal, one in the Free State *platteland* (countryside), four in the rural Cape, and one in the farming districts of Natal. Five years later the two new urban seats were found by eliminating one rural constituency in both the Cape Province and the Free State.

Thus in consequence of population shifts between 1936 and 1946, eleven new urban seats were created at the expense of eleven rural ones. At least seven of these new seats were taken from those areas of the Union where the HNP was strongest, the rural Cape Province and the Free State. In addition, three others were obtained from the rural Transvaal, where the HNP, though not previously strong, was potentially so. One new seat was created in Durban, wholly beyond Malan's reach, and nine others were situated in urban areas

[4]*Sixth Census* (1936), Vol. I, p. xiii; *Census* (1946), Vol. I, Table No. 6, p. 6.

of the Transvaal where as yet the HNP had failed to demonstrate real strength.

The re-delimitations of 1943 and 1948 thus cost the HNP at least a half-dozen sure seats. Eighty rural seats remained, but perhaps as many as ten of these were in Natal and the eastern Cape Province, where Malan had little hope of making electoral inroads. Thus by 1948 it had become impossible for Malan to become prime minister as Hertzog could have become prime minister in 1929, on the basis of support derived exclusively from the Afrikaans-speaking country districts.[5] Of necessity, Malan had to find unprecedented support in the urban areas if he hoped to come to power.

But if Malan was compelled in 1948 to seek electoral support in the Union's urban areas, his chance of finding such support there had seemingly increased. The migration of whites from rural to urban areas between 1936 and 1948 was primarily a movement of Afrikaners. The 1946 census showed that during the preceding decade the Afrikaans-speaking section of the urban white population had increased from 43.8 percent to 49.5 percent. Indeed, in 1946 there were actually 47,000 fewer Afrikaners in the countryside than there had been in 1936, while over the same period the number of English-speaking persons in the rural areas had actually increased by more than 4,000. The growth of the Afrikaans-speaking section of the white urban population had been greatest in the Transvaal. In 1936 this section had constituted 44.3 percent of the total, but a decade later the figure had risen to 52.4 percent.[6] In the municipal area of Pretoria, for example, Afrikaners constituted 51.5 percent of all whites over 21 years of age in 1936 and 61.3 percent in 1946. Comparable statistics for the Witwatersrand are 29.2 percent in 1936 and 36.4 percent in 1946. The 1946 census figures showed that for the first time, Afrikaans-speaking persons constituted a majority of whites of voting age within the municipal boundaries of Germiston, Boksburg, Brakpan, and Roodepoort-Maraisburg. Moreover, previous Afrikaans-speaking majori-

[5]In 1929 National Party candidates were elected from six urban seats, mostly in the Transvaal.
[6]*Census* (1946), Vol. IV, Table No. 14, p. 54.

ties within the municipalities of Krugersdop and Randfontein had been strikingly increased. The 1946 census also demonstrated an impressive increase in the comparative size of the Afrikaans-speaking population of voting age at Bellville, near Cape Town, and in certain other magisterial districts apart from the large urban centers, such as Witbank in the Transvaal, Vryheid and Klip River in Natal, and Uitenhage and De-Aar in the Cape Province.[7] In each case these were areas of local industrial development.

The net impact of the urbanization of Afrikaners over the decade prior to the 1948 election appears, therefore, to have been to improve Malan's chances for victory in that election. While this process resulted in the elimination of between six and ten HNP seats in the Union's rural areas, these losses were probably more than offset by population changes in the cities that seemed to open the door to possible HNP victory for the first time in perhaps a dozen urban constituencies.

[7]*Sixth Census* (1936), Vol. IV, Table No. 10, pp. 72-75; *Census* (1946), Vol. IV, Table No. 16, pp. 80-83.

7·

Turn of the Tide

CHAPTER FIVE indicated four "positive" attitude forces decreasing the appeal of the HNP in 1943. Combining two of them, these attitude forces can be summarized as party fission; reactionary and politically exclusive policies; and circumstances over which neither the government nor the opposition could exercise much control, but which tended, nevertheless, to bolster the government's prestige — specifically, the course of the war in North Africa and Europe. Five years later, the South African political context was markedly different. Among Afrikaner nationalists, unity had replaced disunity. The war was over, and now the slogans with the greatest popular appeal, most especially slogans about race, appeared to be on the other side. In 1943, according to Roberts and Trollip, "the country balked at the idea of 'swapping horses in mid-stream,' especially when the Prime Minister was a person with the personality and prestige of Smuts."[1] After 1945, the patriotic sentiments of wartime gave way to public frustrations and resentments at the retention of vexatious and badly administered wartime controls, while as in America and Great Britain at the same time, the end of the national exertions of war appeared to give birth to feelings that a change in political leadership was needed. Smuts' prestige doubtless remained high, but even among his supporters the belief grew that his interests lay overseas

[1]Roberts and Trollip, *The South African Opposition,* p. 159.

and in international affairs rather than at home with the practical and daily needs of his own people.[2] In short, attitude forces that were distinctly "positive" in 1943 were nearly as distinctly "negative" by 1948.

Unity

The results of the 1943 election demonstrated that for the moment, at least, there was no hope of political success in constitutional opposition apart from the National Party. Moreover, for those groups that had placed their faith in the expectation of constitutional change in South Africa arising out of a German military victory over Great Britain, the course of the war in Europe from 1943 onwards gave no cause for comfort. Conceivably Havenga and the Afrikaner Party might now come to some understanding with Smuts, but for the Ossewa-Brandwag, the New Order and the other small groups to the far right of the HNP, the only alternative to political extinction lay in some form of reconciliation with Malan.

For their part, the leaders of the HNP were not concerned with the survival of their party, which was now assured, but with its triumph over Smuts. The cooperation of the OB and the New Order in future elections might add slightly to the party's present total of parliamentary seats, but no dramatic increase would be possible without the support of a considerable number of electors who had voted for Smuts in 1943, and to hope to obtain such support, the HNP must now endeavor to achieve a more moderate image. Clearly, this necessary effort would be ill-served by an alliance at this time between the HNP and either the OB or the New Order (or both), save possibly on terms amounting to unconditional surrender. In contrast, Malan could well view some accommodation with Havenga and the remnants of the Afrikaner Party as being wholly consistent with his post-1943 strategy, an achievement all the more to be desired because of its likely inclusion in Smuts' plans.

[2]See, for example, Thomas Boydell, *"My Luck's Still In" (with more spotlights on General Smuts)* (Cape Town: Stewart, 1948), p. 141.

Pirow was one of the first to give public recognition of the new realities of South African politics. Little more than three months after the 1943 election, he proposed a collective security pact among all opposition groups.[3] Realization of such a pact was of the greatest importance to the New Order after 1943, but the HNP, whose own security would hardly be increased thereby, ignored Pirow's suggestion. Further approaches were made in 1944, and to show good faith, Pirow now coupled these with an unconditional promise of electoral support. On June 22 at Benoni, Pirow declared that while the New Order did not believe in the vote, its members would "support Dr. Malan and the Party through thick and thin until such time as the vote is no longer decisive."[4] But all of this was of no use. Pirow had nothing to give Malan at all comparable to the concessions he hoped to extract. Thus rebuffed, the New Order and Pirow had to accept the role of a shrill and increasingly isolated voice deep in the (right) wings of the stage of South African politics.

In October of 1945 Pirow began publishing a weekly news-sheet, *Die Nuwe Orde*. In the opening issue, Pirow defended the right of the New Order to exist as an organized propaganda group *within* the ranks of the HNP, and subsequently there flowed from its pages a continuous stream of gratuitious advice to all opposition leaders, along with extreme right-wing political commentary. On September 19, 1947, the former Minister of Defense was convicted of incitement to commit violence for publishing in *Die Nuwe Orde,* May 9, 1947, an article entitled "Take the Law into Your Own Hands."[5] (Pirow was fined £ 40.) After this, the New Order Group ceased altogether to have serious political relevance, although its news-sheet continued to be published through the time of the 1948 election. On April 8, 1948, at the time of the beginning of the campaign preceding that election, Pirow arrived in Britain "on business" and for talks with his British political counterpart, Sir Oswald Mosley.

[3] *Die Vaderland,* October 18, 1943.
[4] *Die Vaderland,* June 23, 1944.
[5] *Rand Daily Mail,* September 20, 1947.

For Malan, the Ossewa-Brandwag presented a more serious problem than did the New Order, since van Rensburg might be correct in his belief that with demobilization, the ranks of the OB would swell. Yet in April 1944 a by-election at Wakkerstroom suggested that the HNP could reasonably count on the support of individual members of the OB, irrespective of the official attitude adopted by that organization. On this occasion, according to Roberts and Trollip, many members of the OB ignored van Rensburg's instructions to the contrary and collaborated with the Greyshirts, the New Order, and the Afrikaner Party in supporting the HNP candidate.[6] The HNP victory in this by-election not only attested to the rewards of opposition unity but also uplifted the spirits of "reunited" Nationalists around the country, for the obvious parallel with the 1924 Nationalist victory at Wakkerstroom that had heralded the imminent downfall of Smuts could not be missed.

Three months later, an event occurred that seemed to end any possibility that the cooperation in the Wakkerstroom by-election might presage a rapprochement between the two bodies. On the evening on July 20, 1944, six men kidnapped F. E. Mentz, an HNP leader on the Witwatersrand and an MP for Westdene, and beat him severely. The OB was immediately suspected. Malan reacted a fortnight later. Possibly feeling that the Wakkerstroom by-election indicated a general willingness of OB members to desert that organization for the party if faced with the necessity of a choice, and having now a suitable pretext, Malan said he intended recommending to the HNP Federal Council that OB membership be declared "incompatible" with membership in the HNP. He further called upon Nationalists who had not yet done so to "cut themselves loose" immediately from the OB.[7] On September 21, *Die Transvaler* reported that the Federal Council had accepted Malan's recommendation and was calling upon the provincial congresses and head committees of the party to

[6]Roberts and Trollip, *The South African Opposition,* p. 164.
[7]*Die Burger,* August 5, 1944.

terminate the memberships of persons who had not resigned from the OB by a date that would be fixed by Malan.

The immediate and specific impact of Malan's action upon van Rensburg and the OB is not known, but whatever the reason or reasons (and it would appear that there were several), the OB at about the time of the end of the war in Europe in May 1945 seems to have suffered a significant decrease in its membership, organizational effectiveness, and political influence. Eighteen months after the war's end, there was little left of the once powerful and pretentious Ossewa-Brandwag. On December 27, 1946, *Die Burger,* reported that it had been reliably informed that at a meeting of the Grand Council of the OB in Bloemfontein on the previous November 20, J.A. Smith, national organizer of the OB, had disclosed that there was hardly any organization left in the body, that membership fees were no longer being paid, and that laxity was apparent everywhere. On January 8, 1947, the *Rand Daily Mail* said that it understood that the membership of the OB had dwindled to no more than 800 persons.

Early in 1945, the OB responded to its increased political isolation by calling for the creation of a parliamentary united front of all opposition groups, a suggestion strikingly similar to Pirow's proposal of fifteen months earlier.[8] However, the idea was soon rejected by Malan, who stated that it was a demand for recognition of the OB as an independent factor. Havenga and Pirow thereafter did likewise.[9] Pirow's coolness towards the OB's idea of a parliamentary united front is surprising, and it seems likely that had van Rensburg persisted in 1945, some accommodation between the OB and the New Order would have been forthcoming. But for van Rensburg, as for Pirow, the only real escape from the political wilderness in which he now found himself lay in some form of agreement with the HNP. In early 1945 such an agreement seemed wholly out of the question, and over the two-year period that followed, there was little that van Rensburg could do but try to keep his organization intact and wait hopefully

[8]*Die O.B.,* January 10, 1945.
[9]Roberts and Trollip, *The South African Opposition,* p. 169.

for some beneficial change in prevailing political conditions. Such a change did appear to occur in March 1947, at the time of the conclusion of an electoral agreement between Havenga and Malan.

The results of the 1943 election appeared to ordain the immediate demise of the Afrikaner Party. An announcement in *The Star* on August 20, 1943, that the federal organization of the Afrikaner Party would be replaced by a unitary structure, while itself suggesting grave problems of organization, seemed less important than the fact, revealed at the same time, that the Afrikaner Party would not nominate candidates for the forthcoming provincial council elections. Soon after these elections, Malan, speaking to the Cape congress of the HNP at Stellenbosch on November 10, said that the party was open to members of the Afrikaner Party, to whom the members of the HNP "extended their hand." This invitation was repeated by Swart before the Free State congress of the party in Bloemfontein six days later.[10] For the moment, acceptance of it appeared to be the only alternative for members of the Afrikaner Party to reunion with Smuts, which latter possibility Malan clearly hoped to forestall. In fact, the Afrikaner Party continued a formal if shadowy existence. Indeed, little was heard of it over the next twenty-six months. The party held no congress during this period nor did it enter a candidate in any of the by-elections which occurred. It seemed likely that many of its members had accepted Malan's invitation and rejoined the HNP. Nevertheless, in January 1946, the executive of the Afrikaner Party instructed all branches to reorganize before May 1, and on January 15, Havenga, speaking at Kroonstad, said he still regarded it as a duty to serve his people.[11] Thus, despite considerable weakness, the Afrikaner Party remained alive as a meeting-ground for Afrikaners of moderate political beliefs, who felt little sympathy for Smuts' imperial preoccupations but had no liking for the reactionary policies of the National Party.

[10]*The Friend,* November 17, 1943.
[11]*Rand Daily Mail,* January 17, 1946.

Havenga's persistence in sustaining the Afrikaner Party and asserting its distinctive identity after 1943 would appear to have been an expression of his conviction that with the conclusion of the war, the appeal of such a middle road would surely grow. Malan's behavior suggests that he agreed with this view. Demonstrating greater political astuteness in this regard than Smuts, he seems to have recognized that neither he nor Smuts could hope for victory in 1948 without the support of those moderate Afrikaners who, in the postwar period, were likely to look to Havenga for guidance. Having failed by the beginning of 1946 to absorb the Afrikaner Party into the body of the HNP, Malan henceforth sought some electoral union of the two organizations.

On March 5, 1947, *The Star* reported that at some time before the middle of October in 1946, Malan privately conveyed to Havenga an offer to meet for the purpose of discussing a union of their two parties, a communication to which, the paper stated, Havenga did not reply. This offer was repeated (somewhat negatively) by Malan in a speech before the Transvaal congress of the HNP on October 15, 1946. There were no differences in principle between the HNP and the Afrikaner Party, Malan declared. He said that he was not against cooperation with the Afrikaner Party and had no objections to discussions with Havenga on this point, provided the talks were exploratory and did not compromise either side.[12]

For his part, Havenga continued to show no eagerness for a closer relationship between himself and Malan. Speaking at the first congress of the Afrikaner Party in five years, at Bloemfontein on November 28, 1946, Havenga declared that the Afrikaner Party had declined cooperation with the HNP because of its refusal to agree to equal treatment for both sections of the European population.[13] However, the Afrikaner Party was prepared, Havenga asserted, to work with *any group* that stood by "Hertzogite principles."[14] On December 4 in Johannesburg, Havenga told the press that there was

[12]*The Star,* October 15, 1946; *Rand Daily Mail,* October 16, 1946.
[13]*The Star,* March 5, 1947.
[14]*Rand Daily Mail,* November 29, 1946.

"no truth in the rumors of 'toenadering' [rapprochement]."[15] Still, the HNP press continued to speak of union. On December 30, 1946, Die Burger pleaded that bygones be left bygones "so that the parties may unite to fight the election with the cry that South Africa must be saved from the menace of non-European advance."

Students of South African affairs appear generally agreed that in late 1946, Havenga, far from wishing for an alliance with Malan, hoped to achieve some understanding with Smuts that might lead to an electoral union of their two parties. Arthur Barlow has written that the Afrikaner Party made a "tentative approach" to Smuts (no date is given) for collaboration through "Kalie" Rood, the MP for Vereeniging.[16] The matter seems to have been discussed in the caucus of the United Party, most probably in early 1947. I have been told by a participant in these discussions that Havenga's terms were these: a guarantee of as many as eight seats in the House of Assembly for former Afrikaner Party MP's; Havenga's admission to the cabinet; and recognition of Havenga as Smuts' successor as prime minister upon the General's retirement from public life. These terms, if these were they, were turned down by Smuts. Barlow says that the "tentative approach" was "frisked aside with contempt."[17]

There are at least three probable reasons for Smuts' refusal. First, it is clear that Smuts did not feel that a union with the Afrikaner Party was necessary for victory in 1948. Second, Smuts could not agree to Havenga's terms, especially that dealing with his own succession as prime minister. Hofmeyr, the generally acknowledged heir-apparent, despite his frequent public denials of further political ambitions, threatened to resign from the United Party should such an understanding with Havenga be agreed to.[18] And finally, Havenga's refusal to support Smuts' war policy had so lowered Havenga in the estimation of the Prime Minister that even in 1947 it is

[15]Rand Daily Mail, December 5, 1946.
[16]Arthur G. Barlow, Almost in Confidence (Cape Town: Juta & Co., 1952), p. 320.
[17]Ibid.
[18]Confidential source.

doubtful that Smuts could have consented to have him in the cabinet. Indeed, Hancock records that even after the 1948 election, Smuts declined to join with Havenga to bring down the Malan government saying that he could not work with a "lot of Fascists."[19] In consequence, Havenga was thrown back to Malan, for if victory in 1948 for either Smuts or Malan required an alliance with Havenga, such a union for the Afrikaner Party was a prerequisite to survival.

Early in March 1947, Havenga traveled to Cape Town for discussions with Malan. These discussions appear to have been protracted, for an agreement between the two men was not announced until March 21. On this day, the two leaders issued a joint statement to the press that declared that since "no difference in principle or in general policy" had been found to exist between them, it had been decided that cooperation between the two parties might take place for the purpose of ousting the "Smuts-Hofmeyr regime." The statement maintained that both parties would retain their identities and that neither had made demands of the other. A decision on the terms of electoral cooperation thus appeared to have been postponed. Concluding their joint statement, Malan and Havenga appealed "urgently and sincerely to all South Africans belonging to other parties or groups, who agree with them on fundamental issues, to give their support towards the achievement of this object [i.e., replacing Smuts]." The two leaders expressed their hope that thereby "our so much desired national unity will once again be established on a firm and lasting foundation, and that all differences which arose as a result of the war or other circumstances will be buried and forgotten for all time."[20] Just over two and one-half months later, Malan and Havenga commenced a series of twenty-five joint public meetings in the Transvaal. On June 10, 1947, they appeared together on the same platform in Potgietersrust, the first such appearance anywhere in fifteen years.

We now return to the OB. For the Ossewa-Brandwag, the resuscitation of the Afrikaner Party in 1946 and the Malan-

[19]Hancock, *Smuts, Vol II,* p. 513.
[20]*The Star,* March 22, 1947.

Havenga agreement that followed offered a last hope for a return to political influence. Relations between the Afrikaner Party and the OB had never been characterized by the bitterness of the relations between the OB and the HNP. Personal friendships, as the one between Hertzog and van Rensburg, had bridged considerable differences over political ends and political methods. Moreover, both organizations could claim victimization at the hands of the HNP and therein find common ground. In 1946, the chairman of the Afrikaner Party, Conroy, officially invited members of the Grand Council of the OB to attend the national congress of the Afrikaner party in November. P. J. Meyer, on behalf of the Grand Council, did attend and also addressed the delegates. Responding to this address, Conroy stated that the Afrikaner Party had "always watched with sympathy the Ossewa-Brandwag's career when it had stood for Afrikanerdom."[21] In February 1947, at a time when there were already strong indications of the forthcoming Malan-Havenga agreement, van Rensburg privately approached Havenga with an offer of cooperation: "I told him [Havenga] how the OB had been badly thinned. Of that there was no doubt. Nonetheless, we were still tough and active cores in each and every district of the Union. If he were prepared to welcome them as members of his party, I would do my best to persuade them to go that way — although they had become somewhat allergic to party politics."[22] To this suggestion, Havenga appears to have agreed. The Ossewa-Brandwag forthwith executed what it called "Operation Afrikaner Party."

Thus, in March 1947, Malan became an ally not only of Havenga but, indirectly, of van Rensburg as well. The HNP, however, appears to have been wary of the OB. On March 23, *Die Transvaler* called upon the OB (and the New Order), in the light of the Malan-Havenga agreement, to dissolve in the interest of "national-unity," and three weeks later, on April 15, *Die Burger,* having previously ignored the OB, appealed to it to follow the example of the New Order and give unconditional support to the Malan-Havenga "unity-

[21]*Rand Daily Mail,* November 30, 1946.
[22]van Rensburg, *Their Paths Crossed Mine,* p. 256.

front." To these appeals for an unconditional surrender of the OB's role as a factor in South African politics, van Rensburg predictably turned a deaf ear. Instead, the OB eagerly assisted in building up branches of the Afrikaner Party in those areas where its organization had remained effective.

Unable, therefore, to eliminate the political significance of the OB, Malan henceforth worked to minimize it. On August 16, 1947, Havenga announced, presumably in response to pressure from Malan, that the Afrikaner Party would not nominate a member of the OB as a candidate for any eventual Afrikaner Party seat.[23] And on September 17, the Transvaal congress of the HNP resolved to readmit members of the OB to party membership provided that the Grand Council of the OB undertook to cease opposing democratic principles of government, including that practice of government by parties.[24] In time, the Grand Council responded, saying, in part, that the demands of the Transvaal HNP congress could be attributed to a "misunderstanding" since 1941.[25] Meanwhile, the Cape HNP congress had reopened membership in the party to members of the OB who renounced National-Socialism. So long as such individuals remained in the OB, however, they might not become officials of the party, including party candidates.[26]

Malan thus endeavored to appropriate to the HNP such support as the membership of the OB might still represent while remaining altogether free of commitment to the leadership of the OB. Van Rensburg naturally sought to confound this strategy. On September 24, speaking in Pretoria, he pointedly reminded followers that the only party which had agreed to receive them without qualification was the Afrikaner Party. The OB, he said, had entered "that open door in good faith and with gratitude."[27] Van Rensburg appears to have said later that while the OB would support Afrikaner Party candidates, it would retain a "free hand" so far as HNP

[23]*Rand Daily Mail,* April 24, 1948.
[24]*The Star,* September 18, 1947.
[25]*The Star,* November 24, 1947.
[26]*Rand Daily Mail,* April 24, 1948.
[27]*The Star,* September 25, 1947.

candidates were concerned, for on October 7, Malan, speaking at Piquetberg, sharply rebuked van Rensburg for suggesting that OB members in the Afrikaner Party might be untrue to the Malan-Havenga agreement. Malan threatened that "unless we get sufficient guarantee that they will support us I will not be prepared [at the time of allocating seats] to include such members of the Ossewa-Brandwag in the strength of the Afrikaner Party."[28]

Malan's threat ended for the moment van Rensburg's pretentions of political independence for the OB in its relations with the party. For just as a realization of van Rensburg's ambitions depended in the first instance upon his understanding with Havenga, so, too, did Havenga depend upon his agreement with Malan to advance the interests of the Afrikaner Party. Van Rensburg's declarations had appeared to bring this agreement into question. Clearly, if he were forced to choose between Malan and van Rensburg, Havenga would have to choose Malan. Van Rensburg soon moved to obviate the necessity for a choice. Speaking at Paarl, an OB stronghold in the Cape, on November 24, van Rensburg asserted that while the OB had found a "political home" in the Afrikaner party, "the fact that this political home has already entered into an alliance with the other opposition wing [the HNP] . . . eliminates from all well-meaning persons any further friction." Continuing he stated: "We are allies, and you do not fight your allies. You fight the enemy, and the enemy is in the Union Buildings, not in the OB or the Herenigde Party."[29] Nevertheless, at the opening of the Afrikaner Party congress at Brakpan on February 4, 1948, Havenga found it necessary to state: "We have no agreement with [the OB]. We are a political organization and do not subscribe to their ideology; but they are Afrikaners. We do not take responsibility for them as a group."[30]

Thus, by the beginning of 1948, Malan had seemingly bridged the divisions which in 1943 had bedeviled the anti-Smuts forces without at the same time committing the HNP

[28]*The Star,* October 8, 1947.
[29]*The Star,* November 24, 1947.
[30]*Rand Daily Mail,* February 5, 1948.

to policies which would have compromised its ability to appeal to some of those who had voted for Smuts in 1943. Most important, in arriving at an agreement for cooperation with Havenga, Malan had bid for the support of those moderate Afrikaners who had in the past been followers of Hertzog but who, in 1943, had shown no liking for the reactionary policies of the HNP.

Meanwhile, the end of the War had brought an end to the coalition government. In October 1945, W. B. Madeley declared that the goals of the Labour Party could not be realized under the system of private enterprise to which the United Party was pledged and resigned from the cabinet.[31] In the following month, C. F. Stallard similarly resigned. At the opening of Parliament in January 1946, both the Labour Party and the Dominion Party joined Nationalists on the opposition side of the House. At the beginning of 1944, the government's majority had been at least 57 votes. Two years later, Smuts could count on a majority of only 17.

In April 1946, the parliamentary Labour Party itself ruptured. Nearly a year later, one of its remaining MP's deserted Labour's ranks. At the beginning of 1948, the Dominion Party suffered a serious split. Each of these developments in some manner served the interests of the HNP, the first being of the greatest importance. These occurrences will be discussed further when we take up the specific questions of policy which brought them about.

A More Moderate Image

In Chapter Six, I maintained that one of the several factors contributing to the defeat of the HNP in 1943 was its reactionary policy in respect to the continuation of the war and the creation of a republic in South Africa. However necessary the adoption of an anti-war and pro-republican stance may have been for the HNP before 1943, as it struggled for supremacy within the opposition, these positions clearly limited its appeal. Many Afrikaner moderates and surely most English-speaking voters could not subscribe to the views that were expressed by Malan, Swart, and Strijdom in 1942 and

[31] *Rand Daily Mail,* October 31, 1945.

1943. The 1943 election showed that the party had little to fear from such bodies as the New Order and the OB. It was thus clear that whatever significant new support the party might obtain in the future would have to come from the ranks of the Afrikaner Party, and more especially from those who had supported Smuts in 1943. After 1943, therefore, the HNP needed a new image. No longer could it afford to be seen by those whose votes it required as a noisy band of extremists and nationalist fanatics. It had to endeavor to be accepted as a normal opposition party; it had to moderate its views.

With the return of peace in 1945, the war issue naturally ceased to be a question of present national policy. It had, in fact, ceased to be such a question as early as the 1943 election, when few could doubt the inevitable victory of the Allies. After the 1943 election, and certainly after the end of the war, Nationalists seemed content to forget the issue. Speaking in October 1945 on the matter of the wartime declarations of members of the HNP, E. G. Jansen, former Speaker of the House of Assembly, said: "No doubt many foolish things were said ... but allowances must be made for the circumstances of the time. The utterances of individual Nationalists cannot be taken as the policy of the party."[32]

For their parts, the partners of the wartime coalition government understandably lost few opportunities to recall the HNP's opposition to the war. Cartoons of Malan in the English-language press up until the 1948 election seldom failed to depict the Leader of the Opposition grasping a pennant on which were enscribed the words, "Nazis are nice." Wartime statements of the HNP were echoed in Parliament, in the press, and at political gatherings. On May 7, 1946, the Minister of Justice, H. G. Lawrence, dramatically revealed in the House the contents of certain captured German documents and insinuated that they proved Malan had communicated in January 1940 with Hitler's Foreign Minister, von Ribbentrop, through an intermediary, a Mrs. Hans Denk. Enraged Nationalists demanded the appointment of a parlia-

[32] *Rand Daily Mail,* November 1, 1945.

mentary select committee to investigate and report on the incident, and two days later such a committee was appointed.[33] Its report, issued on June 17, exonerated Malan of any wrongdoing,[34] and with this, the political attentions of the public seem to have shifted to postwar issues despite the continued efforts of United Party propagandists to highlight the war record of the Nationalist opposition.

Republicanism might have been such a postwar issue, and, indeed the United Party did its best to make it so. Speaking before the Natal United Party congress meeting at Pietermaritzburg on December 9, 1947, F. C. Sturrock, Minister of Transport, told the delegates: "The Nationalists want a republic. They want to overthrow the Commonwealth. That is the issue, and don't forget it when you are called upon to cast your vote at the general election."[35] But from the point of view of the HNP, republicanism was no more useful a campaign issue now than was the question of South African participation in the war. Malan sought the votes of non-republicans just as he did the votes of those who had supported Smuts' war policy. The HNP had to ignore the constitutional question.

There were two aspects to the republican issue. The first was whether or not the HNP would, if returned to power in 1948, declare South Africa to be a republic. The United Party warned the electorate that such a declaration would probably be made if Malan became prime minister. Malan, however, declared at Worcester in late September 1946 that he would seek no mandate on the constitutional question in 1948, and he emphasized that the HNP constitution stipulated that the question of a republic could only be decided at a special election or a popular referendum and not in consequence of an ordinary general election.[36] Malan's statement, which later became the official position of the party, did not deny that the HNP still looked to the day when South Africa would be transformed into a republic. In fact, HNP leaders often found it necessary to remind their

[33]*House of Assembly Debates,* Vol. 57, 1946, col. 6972ff.
[34]*The Star,* June 17, 1946.
[35]*The Star.* December 9, 1947.
[36]*The Star,* September 28, 1946.

followers that the party had not abandoned its republican ideal.[37] What form the party hoped the future republic might take therefore remained, a pertinent question, if not one of immediate importance. This was the second aspect to the republican issue.

The United Party insisted that Malan had set out his ideas for the future republic in the draft constitution published in *Die Transvaler* and *Die Burger* in January 1942, and government supporters publicly examined every detail of that constitution, giving particular consideration and publicity to the provision that would reduce English to the position of only a second language in South Africa. The response of the HNP to this attack was to repudiate the entire document. On July 17, 1947, *Die Transvaler* emphatically denied that the party had been responsible for the constitution, a contention which gained plausibility when read in the light of a (wrong) statement in *Die O.B.* on January 17, 1945, to the effect that the draft constitution had been drawn up by the Ossewa-Brandwag. HNP spokesmen insisted that the party would respect and maintain the rights of the English-speaking population in South Africa.

Thus at the end of the war, the HNP sought to stand apart from those issues that restricted its electoral appeal, while simultaneously Malan worked positively to broaden his political following. Clearly, Malan's agreement with Havenga in 1947 served this end. And for the first time the party even sought out the votes of English-speaking electors. In February 1945, the party commenced publication on the Witwatersrand of a daily English-language newspaper, *New Era,* so that the principles of the HNP might be explained to those "who cannot read Afrikaans."[38] In 1947, the party selected R. H. Macleod, an English-speaking ex-soldier, to contest a by-elec-

---

[37]*Die Transvaler* pointedly omitted all news of the visit to South Africa by the Royal Family early in 1947, while Malan did not take part in the Address of Welcome to the King by Members of Parliament at Government House, Cape Town, on February 17, 1947.

[38]*New Era,* February 18, 1945. *New Era* ceased publication on April 10, 1947, shortly after its editor, E. G. Jansen, had been elected to the House in a by-election at Wolmaransstad.

tion at Hottenstots-Holland. (Macleod withdrew before nomination day, however, and was replaced by an Afrikaner,
H. J. van Aarde.) In short, the HNP worked to replace its
image as a "nationalist" party with that of a truly "national"
party. Fundamentally, this required of the HNP that it
develop a program with a broad appeal.

The party's initial effort at this task resulted in the formu-
lation of a scheme for social and economic reform. The plan
does not seem to have inspired the interest of the electorate,
however, and in consequence, while it was certainly not
repudiated nor entirely forgotten, it was not vigorously pro-
moted. The party did, as we shall see, attempt to articulate
the social and economic grievances of the (white) public as
they developed during the period of national readjustment
after the war. But it concentrated on specific issues such as
the housing shortage and the inadequate food supply rather
than mounting a general attack on the social and economic
systems.

Race

The HNP was soon compensated for the political failure
of its program of social and economic reform. In 1946 Smuts
introduced legislation giving Indians in Natal and Transvaal
limited franchise rights, thereby raising again the always
politically explosive issue of the Union's race relations. After
this, the race issue remained prominent in South African
politics until 1948, indeed perhaps to the present day. It
provided Malan with his best opportunity to exceed the limits
of his party's appeal, imposed by its character and immediate
history, among color-conscious Afrikaners generally, and
especially among newly urban, working-class Afrikaners
whose support we have already identified as critical from
Malan's standpoint. The special sensitivity of urban Afrikaners on matters of race was discussed in Chapter One.

Smuts had failed to find a permanent means of controlling
Indian purchase of land in so-called "white areas" in Natal
that was acceptable to both the Europeans of that province
and the Union's Indian population. A temporary measure,
the Pegging Act of 1943, was due to lapse at the end of March

1946. Further, the current report of a commission of inquiry (the third Broom Commission) suggested a "loaded" or qualified franchise for the Indian population.[39] Responding, Smuts introduced the Asiatic Land Tenure and Indian Representation Bill in the middle of the parliamentary session of 1946. There were two parts to this bill. The first dealt with land tenure rights and provided that an Asiatic might not exchange real property in Natal with a non-Asiatic except with the permission of the government or unless that property lay in certain exempted areas. The second part dealt with Indian franchise rights. Indians in Natal and the Transvaal were not to be admitted to the common voters' roll, but they were to be permitted to elect three white MP's and one white senator. (The government was to nominate an additional senator to represent the interests of Indians). Also, Indians in Natal were to be allowed to elect two members to the Natal Provincial Council, both of whom might be Indians themselves.

The introduction of the Asiatic Land Tenure and Indian Representation Bill aroused much opposition to the Smuts government in Parliament and outside. White opponents of the bill attacked its franchise provisions and Malan called in vain upon Smuts to dissociate the bill's two parts, suggesting that the HNP might support a bill which incorporated only the government's land tenure proposals.[40] The Indian community meanwhile rejected the bill in full.[41] Nevertheless, Smuts proceeded with the legislation, ignoring another suggestion by Malan that the Pegging Act be extended for two years and the government's measure submitted to a parliamentary select committee.

The result was a momentary political realignment in Parliament which, while it was not sufficient to secure the defeat of the bill, thereafter left the anti-HNP forces weaker and less united. The Dominion Party opposed the measure with no less bitterness than did the Nationalists. This was, however, of no direct, long-term consequence, for by 1946 the

[39]*Report of the Commission of Inquiry into the Indian Population of the Province of Natal,* U.G. No. 22, of 1945, p. 17.
[40]*House of Assembly Debates,* Vol. 56, 1946, col. 4866ff.
[41]Kruger, *Age of the Generals,* p. 218.

Dominion party was already a spent force. Moreover, while the Dominion party might join hands with the HNP on this specific issue, no lasting cooperation between the two parties was possible. United Party MP's from Natal supported Smuts this time most reluctantly. However, the issue split the Labour Party. The Labour Party caucus voted to support the bill, but W. B. Madeley, the leader of the party, and M. J. van den Berg, the Labour MP for Krugersdorp, refused to do so. Both opposed the franchise provisions of the bill and sided with Malan at the time of its third reading. On April 17, 1946, Madeley left the Labour Party benches to sit alone as an Independent. Three months later, on July 23, he formally resigned from the Labour party, and on May 1, van den Berg joined the HNP. In announcing his decision to follow Malan, van den Berg declared that "for the first time in our history the opportunity has arisen where nobody need seek excuses or fabricate reasons for not joining the Nationalist Party."[42]

Other happenings in 1946 and 1947 also drew public attention to the question of South Africa's race relations. On August 12, 1946, 13,000 African members of the offically unrecognized African Mineworkers' Union struck for higher wages on the east Witwatersrand, and on the same day 4,000 strikers marched on the Johannesburg City Hall, where they were met by the police who drove them back to their compounds in West Springs. The strike spread until August 16, when the police finally put it down. Some 60,000 to 70,000 African miners had been involved, making it the biggest strike since the so-called Rand Revolution of 1922. On August 15, African members of the Natives Representative Council called on the government "forthwith to abolish all discriminatory legislation in this country," and then adjourned the Council indefinitely to protest the government's "breach of faith" in putting down the strike of the African mineworkers.[43]

In response to the passing of the Asiatic Land Tenure and

[42]*The Star*, May 1, 1946.
[43]*The Star*, August 16, 1946. For extensive background on the Natives Representative Council, see Margaret Ballinger, *From Union to Apartheid: A Trek to Isolation* (Cape Town: Juta, 1969), especially Part II.

Indian Representation Act in 1946, India immediately withdrew her High Commissioner from Pretoria, severed trade relations with the Union, and accused South Africa in the United Nations of contravening the provisions of the U.N. Charter. And charging that the Union's policies of racial discrimination would adversely affect the inhabitants of South-West Africa, India joined others in successfully opposing Smuts' request to the Trusteeship Council in November 1946 for permission for South Africa to incorporate the Territory.[44] India's hostility toward South Africa at the United Nations contributed to a hardening of European attitudes in the Union on race policy. Increasingly talk was heard of repatriating all 285,000 Indians in South Africa to India, and in the Transvaal a European boycott was mounted of Indian traders. An Indian Boycott Congress, meeting in Vereeniging on March 12, 1947, resolved that "the Indians must be systematically excluded from the economic life of this country, so that it will not be worth their while to remain in South Africa."[45] South African Indians, meanwhile, encouraged by the support of New Delhi, engaged in sporadic acts of passive resistance and boycotted the elections of their new parliamentary representatives.[46]

Early in June 1947, a magistrate's court at Bethal in the eastern Transvaal heard evidence that the working conditions of African farm laborers employed by a local farmer amounted to near slavery. Shortly thereafter, Michael Scott, an Anglican priest, visited the area, and later he disclosed that such conditions were indeed commonplace on farms in the Bethal district. On June 30, it was announced that the government would investigate; the next day the Minister of Justice stated that the police would act immediately to "clean-up" unsatisfactory conditions of African farm labor in Bethal.[47] The Bethal farmers themselves heatedly denied the validity of Scott's charges and claimed that the entire district was being

[44]*Rand Daily Mail,* November 5, 1946, and December 9, 1946.
[45]*Rand Daily Mail,* March 13, 1947.
[46]Marquard, *Peoples and Policies of South Africa,* p. 85.
[47]*Rand Daily Mail,* July 2, 1947.

"vilified for the actions of a few."[48] The HNP press appeared to side with the farmers. On July 10, farmers in Bethal gathered and angrily demanded that the police be withdrawn from the district and that a special committee be appointed to investigate conditions of African farm labor there.[49] But ten days later, the Minister of Justice stated that the police reports had "vindicated" the Bethal farmers. Allegations of widespread abuses of farm laborers had been shown to be "unfounded," the Minister said.[50] With this the matter was officially closed, but one may presume that the resentment of the Bethal farmers toward the government was not soon forgotten.

Whatever the life of African laborers on the farms of Europeans (and one can scarcely doubt that some African farm laborers were abused), the living conditions of the urban population at the end of the war were clearly unsatisfactory. Reasons for this were undoubtedly several, the low wages paid to most Africans being one of the more obvious. Another cause was certainly the considerable increase in the size of the urban African population during the war. At the beginning of the war, the Minister of Native Affairs, Deneys Reitz, suspended enforcement of the urban influx regulations affecting the movement of Africans from the countryside to the cities.[51] The 1946 Census showed that during the preceding decade the number of Africans in the Union's urban areas had increased by 547,000 persons, or by 47 percent.[52] In 1946, indeed, there were nearly as many Africans in the urban areas as there were whites. Yet at the beginning of the war, construction of facilities for Africans living in the cities had virtually ceased, and in consequence, established residential areas for urban Africans deteriorated greatly and African "squatters-camps" grew up in vacant land around most of the Union's urban centers. Conditions of residence for most

[48]*Rand Daily Mail,* July 3, 1947.
[49]*Rand Daily Mail,* July 11, 1947.
[50]*Rand Daily Mail,* July 21, 1947.
[51]Albert Luthuli, *Let my people go: An Autobiography* (London: Collins, 1962), p. 245.
[52]*Census* (1946), Vol. I, Table No. 6.

urban Africans in the immediate postwar period were inde-
scribably bad. Moreover, these conditions and their social
results were not hidden from the view of Europeans, or at
least not completely. In 1947 on the Witwatersrand alone,
there were 110 reported assaults by non-Europeans upon
European females, 338 reported murders of non-Europeans,
and 12,204 reported instances of housebreaking and theft.[53]

In August 1946, Smuts appointed a Native Laws Commission under the chairmanship of Mr. Justice H. A. Fagan, a
former "reunited" Nationalist MP, to inquire into the "operation of the laws in force . . . relating to Natives in or near
urban areas," the pass laws and the employment in the mines
and other industries of migratory African labor.[54] And on
May 14, 1948, less than two weeks before the general election,
the Secretary of Native Affairs convened a conference of
municipal Native administrators to discuss the "evil" of
peri-urban African squatting.[55] Smuts may have hoped that
the appointment of the Fagan Commission would set South
Africa's race relations beyond the scope of domestic political
controversy, but the Commission's terms of reference were
too limited. Moreover, the Nationalists would not so easily
be robbed of an important issue on which to attack the
government. Addressing the Free State HNP Congress on
October 17, 1946, Swart said that the time had come for a
"showdown" with Smuts on the color question.[56]
    Yet in the months which followed, the suggestion was often
made that South Africa's race policies should not be allowed
to become a political issue. This suggestion originated in
different quarters, and the means proposed whereby questions
of race relations might be removed from politics varied. In
November 1946, the Labour Party issued a statement which
called for a national convention of all parties for the purpose
of framing an agreed "non-European policy."[57] At the end

[53]House of Assembly Debates, Vol. 62, 1948, cols. 818-819.
[54]Union of South Africa, Department of Native Affairs, Report of
the Native Laws Commission 1946-48, U.G. 28, of 1948, p. 1.
[55]The Star, May 14, 1948.
[56]Rand Daily Mail, November 18, 1946.
[57]Rand Daily Mail, November 29, 1946.

of January 1947, Senator Basner, one of the four senators representing African interests, called for a national convention of representatives of all racial groups to arrive at a national race policy, the results of which convention would be submitted to the United Nations for its approval. The same day, Senator van Niekerk (HNP) called for the creation of a joint committee of both Houses of Parliament to devise a "comprehensive color policy for the Union based on the principles of separation."[58] And on May 20, 1947, Tom Naude, an HNP front-bencher, said in the House that the only hope South Africa had of solving its race problem lay in taking the issue out of the "political field" and appointing a commission or a select committee composed of men "experienced in all aspects of Native affairs" to consider the matter.[59] From all these proposals Smuts and the United Party turned away.

But if Smuts was unwilling to turn over the task of drafting a comprehensive race policy for South Africa to a national convention, a parliamentary select committee, or some other ostensibly nonpartisan body, Smuts' political enemies were ready to take the initiative and apply themselves to this effort. Already in 1944, the "national-minded" Federasie van Afrikaanse Kultuurverenigings (Federation of Afrikaans Cultural Organizations) had convened a Volkskongres on the question of race policy. Three years later, Afrikaans-speaking intellectuals, among them T. E. Donges, E. G. Jansen, N. Diederichs, and A. C. Cilliers, who had previously been considering informally the question of race relations and had already agreed upon the desirability of a complete territorial separation of the races — apartheid — met in Stellenbosch and founded Die Suid-Afrikaanse Buro vir Rasse Aangeleenthede (The South African Bureau of Racial Affairs), or SABRA.[60] Also in 1947, the HNP's Federal Council appointed a commission under the chairmanship of P. O. Sauer, MP, to formulate a race policy for the party for use in the forthcoming election.

The results of two by-elections held in 1947 seemed to suggest that Smuts was indeed vulnerable on the question

[58]*Rand Daily Mail,* January 31, 1947.
[59]*Rand Daily Mail,* May 21, 1947.
[60]Walker, *A History of Southern Africa,* p. 770.

of race policy. The HNP fought both by-elections on this issue. The first was held at Hottentots-Holland, a partially urban seat on the outskirts of Cape Town, in January. Smuts called upon the electorate to give him an expression of confidence in his recent (and personal) conduct of South Africa's defense before the United Nations, but on the eve of the election, Hofmeyr, speaking on behalf of the United Party's candidate, revealed his own conviction that Africans and Indians would inevitably come to represent themselves in South Africa's legislative bodies.[61] The by-election result was a victory for the HNP, the first victory ever for the party in this constituency that only three and one-half years earlier had returned a United Party candidate with a majority of 1,288 votes. The HNP's majority in this instance was 637 votes.

The victory of the HNP candidate two months later at Wolmaransstad was not in itself surprising. This by-election was necessitated by the death of J. C. G. Kemp, co-leader of the HNP in the Transvaal. Except in 1938, Wolmaransstad had not failed to return a Nationalist, of whatever variety was current at the time, since 1915. However, in 1947, the HNP increased its majority by 1,377 votes.

Thus at the beginning of 1948, it was clear that Malan would follow the example of Hertzog in 1929 and contest the forthcoming election on the "Black Peril" issue. At the opening of Parliament on January 16, Malan as the Leader of the Opposition declined to move the customary motion of no-confidence in the government, but instead placed before the House a resolution calling for the elimination of African and Indian representation in the House of Assembly and for abolition of the Natives Representative Council. From Malan's standpoint, the response of the parliamentary parties to this resolution could only be taken as a good omen. Predictably, the United Party and the Labour Party opposed the resolution and succeeded in defeating it, but C. F. Miles-Cadman, who had left the Labour Party in March 1947

[61]Tom Macdonald, *Jan Hofmeyr: Heir to Smuts* (Cape Town: Hurst and Blackett, 1948), pp. 197-198.

alleging that it had become subject to "strong Communist influences" and thereafter formed the Central Group, voted with Malan. Later, Miles-Cadman stated that although the Central Group sought to preserve the existing constitutional position of the country, on Native policy it was closer to the HNP than it was to Smuts.[62] C. F. Stallard also supported Malan this time. This had the result of splitting the Dominion Party, for on January 26, J. S. Marwick, MP for Pinetown, and Senators Stubbs and Richards announced that they disagreed with Stallard's race policies and were therefore resigning from the party.[63]

The next day Stallard issued a statement in which he said: "The time has come when those who think alike [on the color question] should get together as they did during the war and subordinate their differences."[64] To which Malan replied: "It [Stallard's statement] is a most striking affirmation of the fact that the point of view of the Nationalist Party towards the colour question is shared by important sections in all other parties and, in fact, by English-speaking together with Afrikaans-speaking people."[65]

Communism

Another theme of HNP propaganda between the end of the war and the 1948 election was the threat to South Africa presented by international communism. Even before the end of the war, in February 1945, Malan had condemned Smuts and the western Allies for accepting the terms of the Yalta Agreement which, in Malan's view, presaged communist domination of all of Europe. For the most part, however, the HNP addressed its attentions to alleged communist advances within South Africa. During the third week of September 1945, a Union congress of the HNP was held in Johannesburg with the theme, "Save South Africa from the

[62]*Rand Daily Mail,* January 21, 1948.
[63]*Rand Daily Mail,* January 27, 1948.
[64]*Rand Daily Mail,* January 29, 1948.
[65]*Rand Daily Mail,* January 30, 1948.

Communist Danger."[66] In early 1948, Smuts himself frequently found it necessary to warn the nation that the behavior of the Soviet Union threatened the peace, for which "strong attitude" the Prime Minister was complimented by Malan. But as far as the internal conditions of South Africa were concerned, Smuts said that communism was a "trivial thing."[67]

In fact, the HNP often linked the "Red Menace" and the "Black Peril." Early in 1948, the party's "Enlightenment Service" published — significantly in both English *and* Afrikaans — a pamphlet written by Eric H. Louw entitled *The Communist Danger.* In this document Louw set out the party's objection to the communist ideology. Communists believed in racial equality and miscegenation, Louw stated, and moreover, they were atheists. Communists thus were a threat to the survival of both white civilization and Christianity in South Africa. Louw claimed that the communists were spreading their propaganda among Africans in the Union, and he accused the government of having closed its eyes to this "menace." According to Louw, the Prime Minister was willing to "let things develop." Smuts and Stalin are "comrades," Louw wrote, a reference to the fact that during the war Smuts had often expressed his high regard for the efforts of the Soviet Union.

On March 15, 1948, the general election having already been announced for late May or early June, Malan attacked the government not only for neglecting the communist "menace" but for its friendly attitude alleged communist-front organizations, notably the Springbok Legion, an organization of ex-soldiers that was as violently anti-HNP as it was pro-government. Malan reminded the House this day that the preceding September Smuts had opened a conference of the Legion and has asked it to help him oppose the HNP in the next election. Malan also revealed that the Minister of Justice, H. G. Lawrence, had been a patron of the Society of Friends of the Soviet Union, together with two other United Party MP's. Finally, the leader of the Opposition charged

---

[66]*Rand Daily Mail,* September 19, 1945.
[67]*House of Assembly Debates,* Vol. 63, 1948, cols. 3190, 3214.

that a number of trade unions were affiliated with the Communist Party, and he specifically called Mrs. Jessie MacPherson, ex-chairman of the Labour Party and a recent mayor of Johannesburg, a "well-known Communist."[68] The timing was superb; the next day the United Party and the Labour Party announced that they had come to an election agreement.

Miscellaneous Government Difficulties:

The end of World War II marked a turning point in the political fortunes of the Smuts government. Previously, most South Africans willingly experienced personal inconvenience and hardships in the interests of the country's war effort, or so it seemed, and the coalition government could count on the war to rally the electorate, or at least a sizable majority of it. But with the coming of peace in 1945, the war issue fell away despite the continuing attempts of the United Party to revive discussion of the record of the HNP in those years. And as we have seen, the coalition itself soon broke apart with the departure first of the Labour Party and then of the Dominion Party for the opposition side of the House. Henceforth, the postwar United Party government was faced with many trying problems arising out of South Africa's readjustment to peacetime conditions, and its handling of these problems created political issues that were far more politically dangerous to Smuts than the war issue which they now substantially replaced in the attentions of the voters.

The government's efforts at its first postwar task, the return of the soldiers to civilian life, did not give birth to significant political controversy. The government's demobilization program was a substantial success, the inevitable petty grievances of a few individuals notwithstanding. But less successful were government programs for dealing with the postwar problems of South Africa's white civilian population, some of which problems were necessarily accentuated by the demobilization of members of the Union Defense Force. Shortages were the principal difficulty, particularly shortages of housing

[68]*Ibid.*, col. 3214.

and of foodstuffs. In its handling of these problems, the government seldom demonstrated impressive administrative competence. Forthright action was commonly delayed by the workings of a cumbersome bureaucracy, while some government promises went unfulfilled, to the delight of the opposition and the exasperation of the public. Indeed, government administration often appeared to perpetuate and even increase difficulties instead of eliminating them, adding as well obnoxious official regulations and controls.

Housing was a particular source of grievance. South Africa's war effort necessarily curtailed the construction of private dwellings after 1939, to the detriment of housing conditions for the Union's civilian population. In February 1944, the Social and Economic Planning Council reported that there existed a shortage of 30,000 homes for whites and 120,000 homes for nonwhites, and it made recommendations for the improvement of offical machinery for dealing with the housing situation.[69] In consequence of this report, the government shortly enacted the Housing (Emergency Powers) Act, No. 45 of 1944, that gave the Governor-General the power to make regulations affecting the building industry. This was followed by the Housing Amendment Act, No. 49 of 1944, that created the National Housing and Planning Commission with power to erect dwellings and purchase and allocate building materials. Moreover, the government soon agreed with local authorities on a new formula for the financing of sub-economic housing that committed it to burden a larger share of the loss in the construction of such dwellings.

Cabinet ministers now spoke confidently of the government's ability to solve the housing crisis. On September 15, 1944, H. G. Lawrence boldly predicted that the government would build 12,000 dwellings in the next twelve months,[70] and ten months later, the same minister announced that "we can clear up the European housing problem in the next twelve or eighteen months," a boast he repeated upon laying the

[69]Union of South Africa, Department of Public Health, *Report of the National Housing and Planning Commission*, U.G. 43/45, p. 1.
[70]*Rand Daily Mail*, September 16, 1944.

cornerstone of the first state-built house on September 3.[71]
Dr. H. Gluckman, Minister of Public Health, revealed at
Worcester on November 2, 1946, that the National Housing
and Planning Commission had been instructed to build 6,000
homes by June 1948, one-half of this number to be completed
by the end of July 1947.[72]

The subsequent housing record of the Government caused
it considerable embarrassment. Far from having solved the
housing problem in twelve to eighteen months after the
middle of 1945, Gluckman had to announce in Parliament
in February 1947 that 36,000 houses for Europeans and
120,000 houses for non-Europeans were still needed.[73] In 1947,
the government issued a White Paper entitled "National
Housing: Review of Progress and Policy." This document
revealed that over a period of twenty-nine months up to the
end of December 1946, the government and government-sponsored agencies had engaged to build fewer than
24,000 homes, at least 6,156 of which remained to be completed
on January 1, 1947. And in sixteen months, nearly half the
time allocated for its construction of 6,000 homes, the National Housing and Planning Commission had completed only
727 dwellings, although work was already underway on a
further 900.[74] On June 2, 1947, Gluckman conceded that the
Commission had not yet built 2,000 homes. Even the usually
pro-government press began to complain of the government's
inability to deal successfully with the housing crisis.[75] The
situation was little improved by March of the following year,
when the Minister of Public Health told the House that in
three and two-thirds years, the government had succeeded
in building only 33,045 homes, 20,000 of these being sub-economic dwellings built for the most part for non-whites.
Moreover, the National Housing and Planning Commission,
now within three months of its deadline, had still not built

[71]*Rand Daily Mail,* September 4, 1945.
[72]*House of Assembly Debates,* Vol. 63, 1948, col. 3788ff.
[73]*House of Assembly Debates,* Vol. 61, 1947, col. 6315.
[74]"National Housing: Review of Progress and Policy," Government
White Paper, Ans. 558 of 1947, pp. 24-27.
[75]See *The Cape Argus,* February 19, 1947; and *The Star* April 8
and May 16, 1947.

3,000 homes. Gluckman pointed out that private enterprise was constructing homes at the rate of 1,000 per month.[76] Nevertheless, by its own calculations, the government had fallen far short of meeting the housing needs of the country. At the time of the general election of 1948, many thousands of voters were still living in inadequate quarters. Significantly, housing conditions were the worst in the Union's urban areas.

Foodstuffs were also a problem. As did most other countries at the same time, the Union experienced shortages of foodstuffs during the immediate postwar period. Although South Africa's capacity to supply its own food requirements was certainly greater than that of most of the countries of war-ravaged Europe, supplies of grains, meat, sugar and vegetables often proved to be inadequate. The situation was made worse by a disastrous drought in 1946-1947 which affected the southern and western grazing areas and ruined the maize crop. And in early 1947, an outbreak of foot-and-mouth disease in Bechuanaland temporarily suspended imports of cattle from the Protectorate. At the war's end, the government did not remove its wartime price controls on food nor cease its regulation of foodstuffs. It thus incurred the displeasure of South African farmers who were unable to profit fully from the inflated world prices for food. Government subsidies to agriculture did not wholly compensate the South African farmer for his restriction to a regulated domestic market. But neither did the government employ a general rationing of food. (Gasoline was rationed until March of 1946.) Hofmeyr announced the government's intention to introduce such a general rationing in a speech on May 14, 1946,[77] and in the months that followed, the necesary and elaborate machinery was established, at a total cost of over £278,000. But on March 25, 1947, general rationing of food having not yet begun, the Minister of Finance stated that a marked improvement in the South African economy had now obviated the need for rationing.[78]

[76]*House of Assembly Debates,* Vol. 63, 1948, cols. 3991-3994.
[77]*The Star,* May 14, 1946.
[78]*House of Assembly Debates,* Vol. 61, 1947, cols. 6488-6491.

There was, however, some official control exercised over the distribution of certain food items. In May 1944, the government began to regulate the flow of meat to the Union's nine larger urban centers, the so-called Meat Scheme. The practice of a "meatless Wednesday" was not suspended until March of 1946, when Smuts called on the public to observe henceforth a "breadless Wednesday." White bread was not regularly available to the housewife until after the general election of 1948. Moreover, the weight of a loaf of bread, when it was available, was reduced by 10 percent. The result was that while postwar food prices in South Africa were only about 40 percent higher than those in 1938 and compared very favorably with food prices in other countries, shortages of certain food items persisted. They were especially frequent in the cities, where waiting in line virtually became a way of life for the urban South African housewife. To a very great extent, responsibility for the food shortages was not the government's, although, to be sure, the public often held it responsible. However, government programs for dealing with the crisis sometimes appeared to contribute to the difficulties. On August 5, 1946, the Select Committee on Public Accounts issued a report that was highly critical of the government's food distribution arrangements.[79] The Meat Scheme proved especially unpopular. Farmers maintained that the application of the Scheme made it pay them to withhold their prime-grade cattle from the urban markets, which they did. In January 1946, the Boksburg City Council called upon J. G. N. Strauss, the Minister of Agriculture, to abolish the Meat Scheme; 300 women raided a government slaughterhouse in Springs; and butchers on the Witwatersrand threatened to strike unless the government withdrew its meat control regulations by January 21.[80] A resolution calling for "a more practical application" of the Meat Scheme was placed before the Cape United Party Congress meeting in Port Elizabeth in November 1947.[81]

[79]*The Star,* August 5, 1946.
[80]*Rand Daily Mail,* January 10 and 11, 1946.
[81]*The Star,* November 27, 1947.

Shortages were not confined to housing and food supply. There was also a shortage of jobs. The annual number of applicants for employment to the Department of Labour from unemployed Europeans increased steadily between 1945 and 1948, from under 76,000 to more than 139,000 for the entire Union.[82] The monthly average of unemployed adult European males for 1948 (2,816; it was 3,163 in 1947) was nearly three times the monthly average for 1944.[83] Still, the number of unemployed in 1948 constituted only a little over one percent of the total number of Europeans who were gainfully employed. The unemployed were concentrated in the cities, however, and approximately one-third were located on the Witwatersrand.

But there appeared to be no shortage of money. On the contrary, inflation was a considerable problem, although no more so than in Canada and less so than in the United States. The retail price index (1938 = 100.0), covering prices of food, fuel, light, rent, and "sundries," rose quickly after the war and stood at 147.8 in 1948. On the average, wages kept pace with the rising cost of living, however. The index of real wages (1938 = 100.0) fell to 97.4 in 1942, but thereafter it recovered, and in 1948 the index stood at 106.0.[84] But inevitably, all did not share equally in the average wage increases. The wages of civil servants, miners, factory, and transportation workers lagged behind the rise in the cost of living, and government cost-of-living allowances, which applied to tens of thousands of workers, fell short of making up the difference. E. S. Sachs writes that the South African Trades and Labour Council, representing 200,000 workers, presented a memorandum to the Prime Minister sometime before the election "emphasizing the widespread and bitter discontent which prevailed among all sections of workers and asking that immediate and

---

[82]*Official Year Book,* No. 24 of 1948, p. 261; and No. 25 of 1949, p. 273. Such applications from work-seekers were made compulsory on January 1, 1947, but this did not result in a sudden jump in the number of applications.

[83]Union of South Africa, *Report of the Department of Labour For the Year Ending 31 December 1947,* U.G. 38, for 1949, p. 11; and *For the Year Ending 31 December 1948,* U.G. 50 for 1950, p. 11.

[84]*Official Year Book,* No. 24, 1948, p. 329.

energetic steps be taken to increase wages and bring down the cost of living." Smuts' response was to invite representatives of the council to come and see him *after* the general election.[85] *The Star* on December 31, 1947, called the rise in the cost of living South Africa's "biggest problem," but a government scheme to reduce the cost of living, known as "REDCOL," was not announced in detail until April 7, 1948. Once again, those most aggrieved were urban residents.

Immigration

It was thus at a time when South Africa was experiencing a shortage of housing, inadequate food supply, and increasing levels of European unemployment that Smuts, on August 14, 1947, announced the intention of his government to embark on a large scale, state-assisted European immigration scheme. Speaking shortly thereafter to the Transvaal congress of the United Party in Pretoria, Smuts said that South Africa needed immigrants to insure its economic and industrial expansion and to maintain its Western civilization, and he spoke of the Union accepting as many as 50,000 immigrants a year. "Let us once more open our doors," the Prime Minister declared.[86]

The reaction of the HNP was predictably hostile. Malan claimed that the Union could not then absorb a great number of immigrants, for the European population was already without adequate facilities. Moreover, the government's immigration policy would compromise the position of the ex-soldiers, Malan said. However, the Leader of the Opposition was probably most truthful when he said that he opposed immigration on the scale proposed by Smuts because it would change the character of the European population, that is, it would "plough the Afrikaner under."[87] Not all of the new immigrants would be English-speaking, but none would be Afrikaners, although Dutch and German immigrants might be expected to assimilate quickly as Afrikaners. In any event,

[85]Sachs, *The Choice Before South Africa,* pp. 44-45.
[86]*The Star,* August 16, 1946.
[87]J. C. Smuts, *Jan Christiaan Smuts* (London: Cassell and Co., 1952), pp. 494-495.

at the rate of 50,000 new immigrants a year, it would only be seven or eight years before the predominance of native-born Afrikaners in the white population would have disappeared, and with it hope of the Nationalists retaining political power.

On February 25, 1947, Malan moved in Parliament: "That this house . . . disapproves of the policy of large scale and State-aided immigration announced by the Prime Minister as being imprudent in concept and disasterous in its consequences. It particularly condemns in the strongest terms the deliberate attempt by the Government in the interests of immigrants, to deprive Union nationals of the protection to which they, as established South Africans, have a natural and indisputable right."[88]

The government proceeded with its immigration program, however, although now Smuts spoke of the possibility of receiving only 10,000 immigrants annually. Still, in 1947, the number of immigrants arriving in South Africa (28,839) was more than twice the number of arrivals in 1946, and in 1948 the figure (35,631) was more than three times as large. Of those immigrants arriving in 1947 and 1948, nearly 88 percent already possessed British nationality,[89] and hence a likely political preference for Smuts over Malan. None of these persons, however, were eligible to vote until after they had been in the country for two years, thus not until after the election of 1948.

[88]*House of Assembly Debates,* Vol. 60, 1947, cols. 32-33.
[89]*Official Year Book,* No. 25, 1949, pp. 1111-1124.

8.

The 1948 Elections

AT the beginning of 1948, Malan and the HNP could look forward to the general election which must come within the year with considerable confidence. Such signs as there had been had given every indication that the political tide was running strongly against Smuts and the United Party. Ten by-elections had occurred since the 1943 election and the HNP had contested six of these. The party had retained Wolmaransstad in 1947, as has been indicated, increasing its majority by 1,377 votes. Three seats had been won from Smuts: Wakkerstroom (1944), Kimberly District (1945), and Hottentots-Holland (1947). The HNP had reduced the United Party's previous majority by 666 votes in a 1946 by-election at Caledon; and, in 1947, the party had entered a by-election at Zululand — which had not been contested by a Nationalist since 1924 — and obtained 1,454 votes for its efforts. Moreover, the parliamentary ranks of the HNP had been further increased by M. J. van den Berg, who crossed to the HNP from the Labour Party in 1946. And in the middle of 1947, J. B. Wolmarans, MP for Losberg, left the United Party for the HNP. E. P. J. Pieterse, MP for Pretoria North-Central, would do likewise on March 17, 1948, after accusing the Smuts government of failing to accord Afrikaans equal standing with English.[1] Still, neither Malan nor Smuts appears to have anticipated that the HNP would increase its parliamentary representation by more than, at the outside, twenty seats at the general election of 1948. It was commonly thought

[1]*The Cape Argus,* March 19, 1948.

that the United Party would be returned to power, albeit with a considerably reduced majority in the House of Assembly.

On March 24, Hofmeyr announced in the House that the election would be held on May 26, but well before this announcement the battle-lines had been given nearly final form. Toward the end of February, Havenga met Malan in Cape Town in order to discuss the allocation of seats to the Afrikaner Party. On September 17, 1947, the Transvaal congress of the HNP had resolved that seats should be allocated between the HNP and the Afrikaner Party as follows: In those constituencies wherein one of the two parties might reasonably hope to win unallied (in fact, this could only be the HNP), that party should select the candidate. In constituencies wherein neither party could succeed without the cooperation of the other, the leaders of the parties should decide which of the two parties would select the candidate. In all other constituencies, no official candidate should be entered, and the leaders should ask their followers to support that candidate who was most likely, if elected, to uphold the race policy of "apartheid."[2] It appears that Malan and Havenga substantially followed these guidelines. Subsequently, it developed that Malan had undertaken to support Afrikaner Party candidates in eleven constituencies. Only one of them, Ladybrand, was by any means a "safe" seat. This concession by Malan was clearly designed to insure Havenga's own reentry into the House. Several others, notably Vryheid, Pretoria-District, Uitenhage, and Vryburg, were clearly marginal seats and, in view of the growing unpopularity of the government, likely to be won by the Afrikaner Party with HNP support. The remaining six, however, would *probably* be retained by the United Party in the absence of a striking turn-over of votes.

The selection of HNP and Afrikaner Party candidates proceeded forthwith, and almost immediately there developed a source of friction between the two electoral partners. To stand as a candidate at Brakpan, the Afrikaner Party nomi-

[2]*The Star,* September 18, 1947.

nated B. J. Vorster, a future prime minister, and at Roodepoort, Louis Bootha. Both individuals were members of the Head Committee of the Afrikaner Party, but both were also prominent members of the Ossewa-Brandwag. Their nominations were thus in conflict with the earlier undertaking of Havenga that the Afrikaner Party would not nominate members of the OB. Malan promptly vetoed both nominations.[3] Bootha now withdrew at Roodepoort and was replaced by J. H. Grobler, a former New Orderite. Vorster, however, insisted on standing at Brakpan as an independent, and the Afrikaner Party declined to nominate a second candidate to stand against him. In the general election Vorster lost to A. E. Trollip, the United Party's candidate, by only four votes. (Thirteen years later both Vorster and Trollip would sit together in the cabinet of Dr. H. F. Verwoerd, and later Trollip would serve as Vorster's Minister of Information.)

The OB responded to these developments in early April by issuing a confidential circular stating that members of the OB were being "persecuted" by the HNP and, as *Die Transvaler* critically observed on April 13, hinting broadly that OB's should refrain from voting for HNP candidates at the general election.[4] On April 17, van Rensburg asserted at Klerksdorp that the OB was prepared to support the HNP in the general election only if the party ceased its opposition to the OB.[5] As many members of the OB were also members of the Afrikaner Party, van Rensburg thus appeared at the eleventh hour to call into question the validity of the Malan-Havenga agreement. Havenga soon demonstrated that he was no longer willing to be an instrument in van Rensburg's now tiresome political strategy. On April 20, Havenga curtly announced at Ladybrand that those OB's who could not support the agreement between the Afrikaner Party and HNP must resign from the Afrikaner Party.[6] Henceforth, the OB was left to maneuver its questionable political forces independently as best it could.

[3]*The Cape Argus,* March 19, 1948.
[4]*Rand Daily Mail,* April 14, 1948.
[5]*The Cape Argus,* April 19, 1948.
[6]*The Cape Argus,* April 21, 1948.

On May 1, the executive of the Grand Council of the OB resolved that OB members should be encouraged to support only those HNP candidates who declared publicly that they would oppose discrimination against the OB "as embodied in . . . the attitude of the HNP leadership."[7] Sometime later, van Rensburg said that the OB had "simply by-passed the [HNP] leadership on this occasion" in an effort "to seek a wiser and less hostile attitude from the [party's] followers."[8] The OB shortly announced that HNP candidates had met its terms in thirteen constituencies, most being seats in the western and northern Transvaal and in the northern Free State.[9] On May 9, however, Malan forbade HNP candidates to make local agreements with the OB which, he said, constituted "infiltration of the Party from the outside." Malan patiently stated that he harbored no "enmity" towards the Ossewa-Brandwag but was "divided" from it by its "unacceptable and foreign ideology."[10] Responding, van Rensburg stated in Pretoria on May 15 that "if it may help to bring about cooperation, we can declare publicly that at no stage has our movement been National-Socialist, nor has it affirmed that ideology as such."[11] To this announcement Malan did not vouchsafe a reply. With few exceptions, HNP candidates heeded Malan's warning and risked the loss of the support of members of the OB. For his part, van Rensburg now had no choice but to attempt to withhold the voting strength of the OB from a great majority of HNP candidates.

Meanwhile, the United Party and the Labour Party arrived at an electoral truce. It appears that the HNP worked to prevent such an agreement, hoping that the appearance of candidates of both parties in certain urban constituencies might allow the HNP to win some such seats with but a plurality of the total vote. In June 1947, J. H. Steyl, HNP Assistant Secretary on the Witwatersrand, declared that the Labour Party was "much stronger than most people think"

[7]*The Star,* May 3, 1948.
[8]*The Star,* May 11, 1948.
[9]*The Star,* May 10, 1948.
[10]*Ibid.*
[11]*The Star,* May 15, 1948.

and could win as many as twenty seats in the next election.[12] However, two by-elections on the Witwatersrand in 1947 demonstrated that the United Party and the Labour Party had a temporary electoral understanding — the United Party did not enter against the Labour Party at Benoni while, in turn, the Labour Party did not oppose the United Party at Langlaagte. Then, on March 16, 1948, the two parties announced an electoral agreement "with the sole purpose of ensuring that the Nationalist Party and its various allies will not be in a position to win seats on a minority vote."[13] In terms of the agreement, Smuts undertook not to oppose the Labour Party in eight seats — six in the Transvaal and two in Natal.

The House was dissolved on April 15, at which time its composition, by seats, was as follows:

United Party	89
Reunited National Party	48
Labour Party	6
South African Party	3
Central Group	1
Independents	2

One seat, George, had been vacant since the death of A.J. Werth (HNP) early in 1948. In addition, there were three MP's representing Africans in the Cape Province who were unaffected by the dissolution of Parliament as their seats were filled at prescribed intervals of five years.

Nomination day followed nine days later, April 26, at the close of which 304 candidates had been nominated in the 150 constituencies. Twelve of these were unopposed and were declared forthwith elected, including only S.P. le Roux at Oudtshoorn for the HNP.[14] The HNP nominated 92 candidates and the Afrikaner Party 10. The total number of HNP-AP candidates, 102, was 8 fewer than the number of HNP candidates in 1943 and even 1 less than the number of HNP candidates in 1938. This decrease was a reflection of the loss through re-delimitation of HNP seats in the rural

[12]*Rand Daily Mail,* June 24, 1947.
[13]*The Cape Argus,* March 16, 1948.
[14]The remaining eleven were all of the United Party.

areas of the Cape, Transvaal and the Free State, but it was also probably a product of a desire of the HNP in 1948 to concentrate its energies in seats it might have a good chance to win. Twenty-six of the seats entered by the HNP-AP Alliance were in the urban centers of the Transvaal, 18 being along the Witwatersrand and 8 in Pretoria.

The Campaign

Although all of the parties had in fact been making preparations for the election since early 1947, the campaign preceding the general election of 1948 may well be said to have begun on March 28. On that day Malan issued the first of a two-part statement on the question of the party's race policy (the second part was issued the next day).[15] This statement was a summary of the report of the HNP's commission on the color question, the so-called Sauer Commission. The commission had concluded that white South Africa faced a choice between "integration and national suicide," on the one hand, and "apartheid" and the protection of a "pure white race," on the other.[16] Not surprisingly, the commission chose apartheid, and now the party did so as well.

The purpose of Malan's statement was to give meaning to the word apartheid in the context of South African race relations, and hence to define the color policy of the HNP, for the term itself is only the Afrikaans expression for "apartness" or "separation." Apartheid, Malan announced, meant the following: outlawry of marriages between whites and non-whites; abolition of the Natives Representative Council and African representation in the House of Assembly and the Cape Provincial Council; recognition of the Native reserves as the true African "homelands" and strict control of African influx to the cities; segregation of whites and non-whites to the maximum extent possible wherever the two groups necessarily come together; protection of European

---

[15]*Die Burger,* March 29, 30, 1948.
[16]*Verslag van die Kleurvraagstuk-Kommissie van die Herenigde Nasionale Party.*

workers from the competition of Africans; and disallowance of African trade unions.

As to the other non-whites, Malan's statement indicated the Coloureds should have a middle position between both whites and Africans: they, too, ought to be protected from the "unfair" competition of Africans, but an HNP government would abolish the common roll Coloured franchise and instead allow the Coloureds to elect three whites to the House of Assembly and another three to the Cape Provincial Council. Indians, however, were a "foreign element" in South Africa, the statement read, and therefore further Indian immigration should be stopped and Indians already in the Union repatriated to India. In the meantime, an HNP government would end the Indian franchise by revising the Asiatic Land Tenure and Indian Representation Act of 1946.

The HNP's formal election manifesto was not published until April 21.[17] It gave first place to the charge that the Smuts government had been both indifferent and impotent in the face of the color problem. Then, in order, the manifesto spoke of communism, the sacrifice of the Union's interests in foreign trade and external relations, and domestic maladministration. On the matter of the creation of a republic, the document reiterated that this question was not at issue in the election and could be decided only at a special referendum. The election manifesto concluded by asking the electorate to decide on the "Apartheid principle" and promised that if the voters accepted apartheid, the party would make a "further effort" in cooperation with all parliamentary parties to define the "scheme" in detail.

Five days later the election manifesto of the United Party appeared.[18] It said that the first object of the United Party was the "maintenance of white civilization and the way of life known as Western Democracy, with unswerving opposition to Fascism, Naziism, Communism and all other forms

[17]*The Cape Argus,* April 21, 1948. The Afrikaner Party appears not to have issued its own election manifesto and to have been content to follow the lead of its electoral partner during the campaign. Indeed, little was heard of the Afrikaner Party during the campaign outside of the ten constituencies that it contested.
[18]*Rand Daily Mail,* April 26, 1948.

of undemocratic government." Other objects were: the achievement of "national unity;" maintenance of the Union's existing constitutional position and economic system; continuation of controlled and selective immigration; enlargement of the rights and functions of the Natives Representative Council; and recognition of the Coloureds as an "appendage" of the European community. The manifesto merely "affirmed" the Asiatic Land Tenure and Indian Representation Act and promised that a new United Party government would "cope" with the rising cost of living. The UP desired to see a stable African labor force, the statement continued, and these persons should be accommodated in parallel urban townships within which they should exercise local self-government.

The campaign itself did not produce new or unexpected issues, though Smuts' recognition of the State of Israel on May 24 may have cost him a few votes of persons who were bitter at the loss of British lives to Palestine terrorists.[19] The government stood on its "not wholly defensible record"[20] and proposed, at the most, adjustments in the pattern of South African race relations. The Native Laws Commission (the Fagan Commission) had presented its report in February.[21] On May 17, Smuts told a Johannesburg audience that the government would carry out the commission's recommendations.[22] Smuts thus brushed aside the objections of several professors at the University of Stellenbosch who only two days earlier had disputed the commission's finding that the influx of Africans to the cities was a necessary economic phenomenon and could not be reversed.[23] The Fagan Commission said that government policy should accept "that European and Native communities . . . will permanently exist side by side" in the cities, bound together by economic ties.[24] Indeed, the overall political impact of the publication of the

[19]Walker, *A History of Southern Africa,* p. 772.
[20]*Ibid.*
[21]U.G. No. 28, of 1948.
[22]*Rand Daily Mail,* May 18, 1948.
[23]*The Star,* May 15, 1948.
[24]U.G. No. 28, of 1948, p. 20.

Fagan Commission Report appears to have been to increase racial apprehension among whites.

The UP attacked the war record of the HNP and warned that a vote for Malan was a vote for leaving the Commonwealth and the creation of a republic in which persons who disagreed with Malan would have no voice. Apartheid was dismissed as a vague and meaningless conception which would be impossible to implement in any case. The HNP predictably responded by highlighting the alleged 'Black Peril" and playing on the recent social and economic grievances of the public.[25] The government was charged with encouraging Africans to come into the "whites' areas." Speaking on the eve of the election at Caledon, Malan said that Africans were "streaming" into the Western Cape where they were displacing Coloured workers who "deserved preference."[26] On May 17, Strijdom accused the government of doing more for Africans than for whites, for example, in the field of sub-economic housing. In addition, Strijdom said that the inevitable result of the government's policy regarding wages and education was that the Africans would "very soon cease to be barbarians" and this would mean that they would obtain the vote.[27] HNP candidates quoted from a United Party publication, A Guide to Politics, in which it was stated that United Party Policy was "gradually to extend political rights to those ["men of darker skin"] who became capable of carrying out the corresponding duties."[28] Strijdom candidly asserted his belief that "we can only remain a white nation in South Africa if we retain the power to govern," and on another occasion he said that "the Natives outnumber us by four to one, and if we lose our position as masters, we might as well disappear from South Africa." Non-whites, Strijdom charged, were being encouraged to think that they would eventually become masters in the Union. He said that

[25]Except where it is indicated otherwise, the following account is based on HNP campaign literature published for use in 1948.
[26]The Star, May 26, 1948.
[27]The Star, May 18, 21, 1948.
[28]United Party, A Guide to Politics for young and old (Pretoria, n.d.), p. 21.

he was opposed to any advancement for Africans.[29]

Smuts' deputy, Jan Hofmeyr, was a particular object of HNP propaganda, for he had never attempted to disguise his own preference for a liberalization of the Union's race relations. The HNP said that after the election it was planned that Smuts would retire from public life and Hofmeyr would succeed him as prime minister. Hofmeyr was accused of favoring political equality of persons of different races and being unconcerned that its "natural outcome" would be "equality in other spheres." It was said that he wanted racially-mixed trade unions, the elimination of the industrial color-bar, and the end of racial discrimination in matters of marriage and adoptions. It did little good for Hofmeyr to say that he did not favor equality between whites and non-whites, for while this statement might be correct, Hofmeyr's attitudes were indisputably more liberal in race matters than those of the overwhelming number of his fellow white South Africans. Moreover, his views were widely known, if little understood. Nor could the public place much importance in Hofmeyr's disavowal of further political ambitions. Smuts would be 78 years old two days before the election. Clearly, the "Oubaas" could not go on indefinitely. And just as clearly, Hofmeyr (age 54 years) would be his successor. No one in the cabinet apart from Smuts could match Hofmeyr's experience and ability. He had at various times held seven different portfolios. During the Prime Minister's wartime and postwar trips abroad, Hofmeyr had served as acting prime minister. In 1946, one such trip had lasted for a period of four months. And at the beginning of the parliamentary session of 1948, Hofmeyr had been formally designated deputy prime minister. On April 20, Malan said at Paarl that "a vote for Smuts is a vote for Hofmeyr,"[30] and an HNP campaign leaflet ended with the peroration, "Vote against Hofmeyr and Save South Africa from Ruin." By his own calculation, Hofmeyr was made the "gogga" (bogey) of the election.[31]

[29] *The Star,* May 18 and 21, 1948.
[30] *The Cape Argus,* April 21, 1948.
[31] *Rand Daily Mail,* April 24, 1948.

The HNP gave scarcely less prominence than that given the alleged color problem to charges of government administrative incompetence and insensitivity. The electorate was reminded of the queues in which the public had been compelled to stand, the much-heralded rationing scheme that was never introduced, the shortages of meat, and the unavailability of white bread. Presumably, HNP propaganda was made more effective in those areas by a momentary lapse in the supply of meat during the first week of May in Pretoria and Johannesburg.[32] Ministerial promises regarding the construction of houses were set against subsequent achievements, to the acute embarrassment of the government. The HNP pointed to persons who were still living in garages and accused Smuts of exporting building materials while shortages of such materials persisted in the Union. The government's immigration program was blamed for taking homes and jobs away from native-born citizens. Official figures of the Department of Labour released after the election revealed that the number of registered unemployed had increased by nearly 1,000 persons — or by 7 percent — during the month of April.[33] Those who might have been concerned about inadequate hospital space were reminded that the Prime Minister had in effect turned down the report of the National Health Services Commission in 1944, saying that "we should not be so idealistic in our plans." The Commission had recommended centralized control of hospital services, in the place of provincial control, and a greater outlay of funds for these purposes.

Strijdom accused Smuts of having sold corn to Southern Rhodesia at below world prices, to the detriment of South African producers. The public was reminded that the national debt had increased from £291 million to £594 million over six years from 1939-1940, or by more than 100 percent. Obnoxious wartime controls that had been continued into the postwar period were recalled, and the government was charged with being helpless in the face of the rising cost of living. It was a sweeping attack on the Smuts regime that took advantage of the variety of public grievances and to

[32]*The Star,* May 8, 1948.
[33]*The Star,* May 29, 1948.

TABLE 1.

RESULTS OF THE GENERAL ELECTION OF 1948

	Reunited National Party	Afrikaner Party	United Party	Labour Party	South African Party	Central Group	Independents and Others
Cape Province							
votes	147,261	9,845	216,475	0	4,180	5,127	25,196
seats	26	2	27	0	0	0	0
Natal							
votes	6,531	7,224	63,970	8,910	6,332	5,485	6,460
seats	1	2	11	2	0	0	0
Oange Free State							
votes	63,045	5,096	29,544 [a]	0	0	0	2,222 [b]
seats	11	1	1	0	0	0	0
Transvaal							
votes	184,997	19,720	215,241	18,450	1,098	5,132	10,678
seats	32	4	26	4	0	0	0
Union							
votes	401,834	41,885	525,230	27,360	11,610	15,744	44,556
seats	70	9	65	6	0	0	0

SOURCE: *The Star*, May 28, 1948.

[a] **Wrongly reported as 28,544. Totals have been adjusted accordingly.**

[b] Wrongly omitted from *The Star's* tabulation.

which, under the circumstances, there could be no adequate political response from the United Party.

The Results

The final results of the general election were not known until early in the morning on May 28. (See Tables 1 and 2.) Moreover, not until almost the last returns had been received from the late-reporting rural constituencies did it become evident that for only the second time in the history of the Union, a government had been removed from office by the decision of the electorate. The morning newspapers on May 27, the day after the election, still had not recognized the electoral defeat that had already been dealt the United Party. In the end, Malan saw his party's delegation in the House increase by 22, from 48 to 70. The Afrikaner Party meanwhile won nine of the ten seats it contested. Together, the HNP and the Afrikaner Party enjoyed a majority of five over the combined total of the Labour Party, the United Party and the three Natives Representatives. Compared with the 1943 results, the Alliance parties increased their share of the popular vote by 7.1 percent, including estimates for uncontested constituencies. HNP majorities in 1943 were increased in every case, and except for A. Davis at Pretoria City, every United Party and Labour MP who faced an

TABLE 2.

EXCHANGE OF SEATS AMONG ALL PARTIES AT THE GENERAL ELECTION OF 1948

Losses	Gains				Eliminated	Totals[a]
	HNP	UP	AP	LP		
HNP	44	1	1		2	48
UP	18	56	7	2	6	89
LP	2	1		3		6
SAP		3				3
Central Group		1				1
Independents		2				2
Vacant	1					1
New Seats	5	1	1	1		
Totals[b]	70	65	9	6		150

[a] Composition of the House at its dissolution.
[b] Composition of the new House.

Alliance candidate was either defeated or was returned with a reduced majority. On May 28 B. J. Schoeman said, "We expected to gain several seats, but nobody thought there would be such a landslide."[34] Four days later Malan exclaimed, "The outcome of the election has been a miracle. No one expected this to happen. It exceeded our most optimistic expectations."[35]

In the Cape, the Alliance vote increased by 6.5 percent. The HNP retained 19 of the 20 seats it had held at dissolution, while Hottentots-Holland reverted to the United Party. In addition, the HNP regained George, which had been vacant, and won at Bredasdorp (and thus unseated the Minister of Native Affairs, Major Piet van der Byl), Victoria-West, Worcester, Malmesbury, Paarl, and Parow. The Afrikaner Party's candidate was elected at both Vryburg and Uitenhage.

In the Free State, the Boshof and Hoopstad constituencies had been combined, and this new division was won by the HNP. The United Party retained Bloemfontein City despite a reduction in the UP's majority of 2,142 votes. Havenga was easily successful for the AP at Ladybrand. The remaining ten Free State constituencies each returned a Nationalist as before. Across the province, the Alliance vote was up by 3.9 percent.

In Natal, the HNP candidate at Newcastle was elected, while the Afrikaner Party was successful at both Vryheid and Klip River. The provincial vote for the Alliance parties increased by 12.0 percent.

The Transvaal results were easily the most dramatic. The HNP retained each of the 15 seats it had held at dissolution and, in addition, won 17 new ones. The Afrikaner Party was successful in 4 others. Of the total of 21 new seats won by the Malan-Havenga Alliance, 6 were on the Witwatersrand where the Alliance vote increased by 12.2 percent, and 3 were Pretoria seats. In Pretoria the Alliance vote was up 8.5 percent. The remaining 12 seats were rural. At Standerton, the result unseated the Prime Minister. The victor, W. C. du Plessis, had left the South African diplomatic service in

[34]*The Star,* May 28, 1948.
[35]*Rand Daily Mail,* June 2, 1948.

1944 rather than resign his membership in the Broederbond to comply with the terms of Smuts' ban on the membership of civil servants in that secret organization. In the rural Transvaal, the Alliance vote increased by 7.9 percent.

Smuts' political humiliation was thus complete, but Malan's victory was scarcely overwhelming. Not only was the new government's majority in the House of Assembly a mere 5 seats at the most, a margin that many commentators thought would be insufficient to maintain it for more than a year to 18 months, but 3 seats had been won by supporters of Malan with majorities under 100 votes, 5 had been won with majorities under 200, and 11 had been won with majorities under 400. (See Figure 2.) A switch favorable to Smuts in the voting preference of as few as 91 electors properly

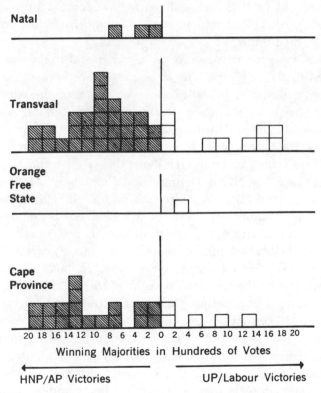

Figure 2. The 1948 General Election. Seats won and lost by the HNP/AP by less than 2,000 votes. (Each square represents one constituency.)

distributed in three constituencies would have kept Malan from power, although in this event Smuts would scarcely have been able to carry on. Further, although the HNP-AP Alliance won 52.7 percent of the seats in the House of Assembly, it received only 41.5 percent of the vote. This low figure was due in part to the fact that the United Party and the Labour Party entered 45 more candidates than did the Alliance parties and received votes in 35 more constituencies. If, however, we make estimates where actual figures are lacking, it seems probable that had the HNP-AP Alliance entered candidates in all 150 constituencies and been opposed in each, the Alliance parties would have received just 43.5 percent of the total vote, though the same distribution of seats among the several parties would have resulted. Malan's government in 1948 was indisputably supported by only a minority of the voting electorate. A majority of all voters had favored Smuts.

This disparity between votes received and seats won requires further explanation. It is not, it can be said at the outset, a result of plurality victories. None of the winning candidates in 1948 secured election with less than a majority of the vote in his constituency because two or more opponents divided the vote against him. It is in part a reflection of the advantage obtained by the HNP and the AP from the practice adopted by the Ninth Delimitation Commission, following the example of all earlier commissions, of "unloading" rural seats and "loading" urban seats. A loaded seat is one having more votes in it than the quota of electors per constituency that is established for all seats in the same province. An unloaded seat is one with fewer votes. In both cases the departure may be up to 15 percent of the provincial quota. The Ninth Delimitation Commission unloaded 68 of the Union's 150 constituencies, and all but ten of these were won by the Alliance parties in 1948. Thus only 21 seats won by the Alliance, but 61 of 71 seats won by its opponents, were loaded constituencies. On the average, there were nearly 600 more voters in seats won by the United Party and the Labour Party than in each seat won by the Alliance. In short, it took more votes to win seats in the areas where the United

Party and the Labour Party won them than it did in the areas of the Union where the Alliance parties were strongest.[36]

Another reason for the disparity identified above is that the HNP-AP Alliance "wasted" fewer votes than did its opponents. A vote may be said to be wasted in either of two ways. One is for it to be cast for a candidate who is defeated. The Alliance expended 77,103 votes in constituencies it did not win, while the various elements of the opposition to the Alliance together expended 319,477 votes on candidates who were defeated. But not all votes cast for a victorious candidate can be said to have been "used." Votes that merely increase the majority of a winning candidate are for purposes of his election superfluous. The number of votes a winning candidate uses is equal to the number of votes obtained by his leading opponent plus one. Thus, the size of a winning candidate's majority minus one is the number of votes wasted by his supporters. The sum of Alliance majorities in 1948 is 108,705 and the comparable figure for the United Party and the Labour Party is 168,823. The United Party and the Labour Party thus wasted 60,118 more votes on winning candiates than did the Alliance, and this figure itself accounts for more than one-half the difference in the total votes obtained by the two coalitions.

Why Smuts Lost

The closeness of many of the Alliance victories in 1948 naturally incites curiosity about peculiarly local circumstances that could have provided the margin of victory in these seats and, in sum, have caused Malan's replacement of Smuts as prime minister. Indeed, and perhaps inevitably, there were such local cirumstances. A marked growth in the proportionate size of the Afrikaans-speaking electorate, unrelated to the re-delimitation of constituency boundaries in 1948, was probably a factor at Pretoria-West and North-East

[36]It is reported by a former general secretary of the United Party that in 1947 the cabinet did consider revising the law governing re-delimitations in the interest of greater political equality among electors. But Smuts and Hofmeyr opposed a majority of the cabinet on this matter, disparaging the idea as changing "the rules of the game," and as a result of their opposition, the idea was allowed to drop.

Rand. Moreover, a similar increase in the Afrikaans-speaking electorate at Vryheid, Klip River, Uitenhage, Parow, Witbank, Germiston, Mayfair, Kempton-Park, Pretoria-Central, Randfontein, and Krugersdorp, while not sufficient to have itself provided the margin of victory, nevertheless explains partially the striking gains made by the Alliance candidates in these constituencies. Within the Uitenhage magisterial district, for example, a somewhat different geographical unit from the Uitenhage constituency, but the only one for which population figures are available, the Afrikaans-speaking population over 21 years of age increased by 2,019 persons between 1936 and 1946, while in the same period the English-speaking adult population increased by only 47 persons. Extrapolating from these figures, and assuming electoral behavior typical for the respective language groups, it seems possible that population increase alone within the Uitenhage magisterial district provided the Afrikaner Party with 573 more votes in 1948 than it provided the United Party. The majority of the winning Afrikaner Party's candidate at Uitenhage was 691 votes.

Local *political* conditions were probably decisive in several constituencies. At Krugersdorp, the HNP candidate was M. J. van den Berg, who had represented that constituency as a Labourite from 1934 to 1946 when he joined the Nationalists. Presumably, van den Berg was the strongest possible candidate for the HNP in this seat. Before 1934, Krugersdorp had been Nationalist since 1921. Yet van den Berg was opposed in 1948 not by a candidate of the Labour Party, as one would have expected, but by a United Party candidate, seemingly a poor choice. This alone may have accounted for a swing of 299 votes to the HNP, enough to provide van den Berg's winning majority of 597. Mayfair, which had returned a Labourite in 1943, was similarly contested by the United Party rather than the Labour Party, and again that appears to have aided the HNP.

Continuing resentment by white farmers in the Bethal district of the government's handling of the 1947 investigation into alleged local maltreatment of African farm laborers may have shifted as many as 421 votes from the United Party to the Afrikaner Party, allowing the latter to capture Bethal-Middleburg by 842 votes. Moreover, this victory and victories of the HNP at nearby Ermelo, Barberton, and Standerton were certainly assisted, and at Standerton probably made possible, by the death of a generation of electors, and with that generation a political tradition of support for the South African Party and the United Party as its successor. This tradition had rested upon personal loyalties to Louis Botha established at the time of South African War and during the Transvaal colonial period that followed. At the end of the South African War, Botha began farming near Standerton and his presence in the eastern Transvaal captured much of that region politically for the South African Party when it was founded. At Botha's death, Smuts, as his political heir, appeared to gain this personal following. With the exception of narrow victories by the National Party at Barberton in 1924 and at Bethal in 1929, Bethal, Barberton, Ermelo, and Standerton never failed to support Smuts in seven successive general elections from 1920. Yet by 1948, Botha had been dead nearly thirty years and Smuts himself was 78 years of age. With the passing of the Botha generation, it was not surprising that the so-called "Botha constituencies" responded politically in a manner more similar to that of other rural Transvaal constituencies. Hancock records that after the 1948 election Smuts exclaimed sadly to a friend, "My old comrades have turned against me." To this the friend replied, "Oom Jannie, how could they turn against you? They are all dead." Hancock observes that "if that reply was comfort of a kind, it was also a devastating truth."[37]

The new-found unity of "national-minded" elements in 1948, though doubtless a factor influencing the results somewhat in all provinces, would seem to have been particularly important in the rural Transvaal. Indeed, this unity alone ought to have produced Alliance victories in at least three Transvaal seats that went for Smuts in 1943 with less than a majority of the total vote. In 1943, persons in the Free State who wished to support neither Smuts nor Malan had the option in every constituency but one of voting for the

[37]Hancock, *Smuts, Vol. II,* pp. 506-507.

Afrikaner Party, but in the Transvaal an alternative to voting for Malan or "for war" was open in only 15 of 64 seats. (The matter does not seem to have been very important in either the Cape or Natal.) As a result, it appears that some rural voters in the Transvaal who might otherwise have supported anti-Smuts candidates in 1943, abstained from voting instead. Their return to electoral participation five years later could be expected to exaggerate the swing to the Alliance parties in this region.

Finally, the 1948 re-delimitation of constituencies appears on balance to have favored the Alliance parties. It will be recalled that six of the eight seats eliminated by the Ninth Delimitation Commission were UP seats. Had these six been retained, the United Party would certainly have held two of them in 1948 and possibly one or two more. As it was, the United Party won one of the eight new constituencies created by the commission and the Labour Party won another. The remaining six went to the Alliance parties. But the redrawing of the continuing constituencies by the commission was probably of more significance to the outcome of the general election. At Kempton-Park, previous UP support was eliminated and added to Edenville, a new seat. The HNP won at Kempton-Park in 1948 with a majority of 900 votes, while a Labourite was successful at Edenville with a majority of 1,419. As many as a thousand railway workers were newly included in the Mayfair constituency, to the probable detriment of the United Party. Mayfair was won by the HNP with a majority of 388 votes. Randfontein obtained HNP support formerly included in the Krugersdorp constituency and, in turn, lost some United Party support to Krugersdorp. The result would appear to have increased the chances of the HNP winning Randfontein (the HNP did win by 894 votes) without seriously jeopardizing the prospects of the HNP at Krugersdorp. The United Party viewed the re-delimitation of Bredasdorp and Klip River as being unfavorable to the government's interests. A Nationalist won at Bredasdorp with a majority of 259 votes, and the Afrikaner Party succeeded at Klip River with a majority of 343.

Local circumstances may, therefore, have allowed for the

election of four to six Alliance candidates (or even more) who would not otherwise have won — in any case, a number sufficiently large to have meant the difference between Malan becoming prime minister or remaining leader of the opposition. Although these factors alone might have been enough to account for as many as ten victories elsewhere, they could not, alone, have resulted in Alliance victories *in these seats*. Alliance successes in the four to six seats we have mentioned were made possible by the *combined action* of a general swing of electoral support to the Alliance *and* local circumstances that served to exaggerate that swing in these constituencies. It was this general swing of electoral support to the Alliance that resulted in the remaining 25 or so constituencies falling to the Alliance, and that was, therefore, chiefly responsible for Malan becoming premier in 1948.

How can we explain this *national* trend? Edward Tiryakian has written that "apartheid won the elections of 1948 for the Nationalist Party," and in another place in the same article he states, "apartheid as a political slogan had carried the day and upset the pre-election odds."[38] This conclusion, that has become commonplace, is doubtless valid in the sense that in the absence of the apartheid slogan in 1948, Smuts would probably have been returned to power, although with a greatly reduced majority. Apartheid can be credited with providing the narrow margin of many Alliance victories, especially in a number of the newly-won urban seats. Indeed, the inordinately great swing to the Alliance parties along the Witwatersrand would seem to owe much to the attitude force of the race issue, and this may have been an especially important factor in Natal as well. In Natal, the ratio of whites to non-whites in 1946 — 1 to 8.3 — was, among all provinces, most in favor of the non-whites, and in Natal, moreover, resentement at the government's Indian policy was the most keenly felt. For Malan in 1948, as for Hertzog in 1929, the alleged "Black Peril" was a politically potent battle cry.

But there were other attitude forces similarly influencing the vote, especially in the cities, and in view of the narrowness

[38]Edward A. Tiryakian, "Apartheid and Politics in South Africa," *Journal of Politics*, XXII, No. 4 (November 1960), 691, 696.

of the Nationalists' victory in 1948, these, too, were critical. Despite the economic prosperity in South Africa in 1948 cited by Tiryakian, public grievances did exist regarding the government's handling of the many problems of postwar national readjustment, particularly with respect to such especially urban problems as housing and meat distribution. Certainly, the Alliance parties made much of these administrative shortcomings in their propaganda, and they were no doubt rewarded for doing so.

Yet, as has been the central argument of this work, there is another, *complementary* explanation for the success of the Alliance parties in 1948, less rooted in the immediate context of the election: the *general* shift of voters away from Smuts and toward Malan was a probable, if delayed, consequence of the break-up of the United Party in 1939. As with Hertzog's victory in 1929, Malan's success in 1948 was dependent upon the exploitation of the issue of race, but there were other similarities as well. Excluding the three Natives Representatives, Malan's majority in 1948 was identical to the majority of the National Party in 1929. Moreover, if it is assumed that all who voted for Hertzog in 1929 were Afrikaners, and if estimates for uncontested seats are included, it can be calculated that their number would have constituted 83.5 percent of the entire voting Afrikaner electorate. This figure is only 0.8 percent higher than the comparable statistics for 1948.[39] Finally, it is notable that with one exception, the locus of Alliance support in 1948 is nearly identical with Hertzog's support in 1929. The major difference is the victories of Alliance candidates in 1948 in five Witwatersrand constituencies that were without precedent in 1929, but this was a probable consequence of the movement of Nationalist sympathizers from the countryside to the cities during the intervening period. It thus seems possible to say that the triumph of the Alliance parties in 1948 was substantially a repetition of the electoral success of Hertzog and the National Party nineteen years earlier.

[39]The method used for obtaining this figure is the same as that employed by J. L. Gray in "How the Nation Voted."

But Fusion in 1934 ended the dominance of the National Party that had been established in 1929 and while it seems clear that Fusion was less popular among Afrikaners than the parliamentary majorities of the United Party up to 1939 suggested, Fusion — and nonpolitical events such as urbanization and industrialization occurring during the years of Fusion — had the effect of increasing social homogeneity, interdependence, and mutual sympathy between Afrikaners and English-speaking persons. Fusion thus saw the erosion of the support of some Afrikaners for traditional Afrikaner values, including those associated with the issue of South African independence. Indicative of this erosion was the fact that four of forty-three pre-Fusion Nationalists in the United Party in September 1939 voted with Smuts in the House of Assembly rather than with Hertzog on the issue of war. Thus when that vote shattered Fusion and ended the United Party (to the extent that it had been a joint political enterprise of Afrikaner moderates and English-speaking South Africans), the partisan alignment that emerged in the early days of World War II probably resembled the alignment that had existed between the Nationalists and the other parties shortly before, rather than at the time of, the general election of 1929. With the support of Labour that Hertzog had enjoyed a decade earlier, Smuts was rightfully prime minister in 1939, but the balance of political forces in South Africa was more delicate than the new prime minister appears to have appreciated. Even allowing for the possibility that political integration of Afrikaners and English South Africans continued after 1939, albeit at a markedly reduced rate, the results of the 1943 election certainly exaggerated the extent of support for Smuts. At the end of the war, some of those "positive" attitude forces that amplified the government's victory in 1943 fell away, while others were consciously eliminated. Therefore, in the absence of (1) a change in the electoral regulations eliminating or reducing the electoral bias favoring the rural areas, or (2) a re-creation of the United Party of the 1930's, or (3) the advent of some other new cast to South African politics, it would seem probable that, momentary political issues aside, Malan would come close to gathering such support at the first postwar election as had sustained Hertzog in 1929 — that is, Malan would show a general advance over his strength in 1943. And should Malan be favored by "negative" attitude forces, it would seem likely that he would become prime minister, even if the electoral influence of such attitude forces were only moderate.

Indeed, there is evidence that does not depend on the argument sketched above that corroborates the conclusion that apartheid and the other issues of the 1948 campaign, while important, are not sufficient explanation for the growth in Nationalist electoral support:

Primarily, it is clear the political tide was running strongly against Smuts and the United Party before 1948, and certainly well in advance of Malan's unveiling of his apartheid program. At the beginning of this chapter, the results of by-elections occurring between 1943 and 1948 were introduced to show a general erosion in government support during these years. Further use of these figures can be made if the by-election results are contrasted not only with the figures for 1943, but with the 1948 results as well. This is possible in five constituencies if the re-delimitation of seats before the 1948 election is ignored, and as none of these was an urban constituency (where small changes in boundaries often mean important differences in neighborhood), there may be little danger in doing this. Table 3 uses the 1943 election as a base-line and records HNP gains as a percentage of the total vote at the 1948 election and at the previous by-elections. It can thus be seen that at Kimberly-District and Hottentots-Holland, the electoral swing against Smuts after 1943 appears to have

TABLE 3.
HNP GAINS OVER 1943 ELECTION RESULTS
(in percent)

Constituency	By-election	1948
Wakkerstroom	6.9 (1944)	14.1
Kimberly-District	5.3 (1945)	4.0
Caledon	4.5 (1946)	6.6
Hottentots-Holland	9.8 (1947)	3.7
Wolmaransstad	12.3 (1947)	13.4

been completed *before* 1948, while at Wolmaransstad and Caledon, the swing against Smuts after their respective by-elections was quite small. Indeed, at Kimberly-District and Hottentots-Holland, there was a swing towards Smuts in the 1948 voting, compared with the results in their two earlier by-elections, and at Hottentots-Holland this swing was sufficient to unseat the Nationalist MP who had gone to Parliament only the year before. (Similarly, at Port Elizabeth Central the government candidate was appreciably stronger against the HNP in 1948 than he had been against an Independent in a 1945 by-election. In 1943, the UP's candidate in this seat was returned unopposed.) Only at Wakkerstroom was the swing to the National Party in 1948 considerably greater than at the previous by-election, but it should be noted that the Wakkerstroom by-election occurred very early, indeed before the end of the war.

Peculiarities of time and place can perhaps be minimized and a more general picture obtained if the results in all five of the above by-elections are summed and then compared with similar totals for the elections of 1943 and 1948. On the basis of such calculations, it appears that 93 percent of the 1948 gains over 1943 registered by the HNP in these five constituencies had already appeared at the time of the earlier by-elections, the last of which occurred in March 1947.

But if by-election results cast some doubt on the electoral value of the apartheid *slogan* in 1948, what about the value to Malan and the HNP of the substantive issue of race? As we have seen, as early as 1944 "national-minded" bodies within Afrikanerdom once again began to exploit the mobilizing potential of the race issue, and certainly it was current in South African affairs from about 1946 onwards. In Chapter Seven it was noted that the HNP highlighted race in two by-elections in 1947. And while Malan's apartheid program was never clearly defined from its first public discussion by the "reunited" National Party until election day less than two months later, as Tiryakian himself shows, there can be little doubt that in 1948 most voters understood that a future Smuts government would follow a path of ad hoc, pragmatic adjustments in accommodating race pressures, while the

HNP/AP Alliance stood for a policy of racial exclusivism in all matters. Yet these were familiar positions on a familiar national problem. As we have shown, except in 1933, every South African general election from 1929 to 1948 highlighted in some fashion the race issue, and throughout this period the support of Nationalists for racial segregation was both clear and steadfast. I want to argue that the primary effect of Nationalist agitation on the issue of race after World War II was not that of realigning partisan preferences but rather that of reinforcing and mobilizing existing Nationalist support, although this is not to suggest that no voters shifted their vote to the HNP for this reason.

What data can be adduced to support this contention? In the absence of political polls (even now not established features of politics in South Africa), it is hard to avoid speculation. Still, V. O. Key has suggested that "critical elections" are characterized by intense and deep involvement on the part of the electorate, and in a similar vein, Campbell and his co-authors of *The American Voter* point out that a "great national crisis" has usually been the immediate context of "realigning" elections in the United States. But in 1948 the South African electorate did not show unusual electoral involvement. Indeed, while the average poll was 3.1 percentage points higher in seats contested by the Alliance parties than in all seats — a result the United Party's general secretary later attributed to the complacency of government supporters that the opposition contrived to instill, the average poll in constituencies that had an Alliance candidate — 82.8 percent — was actually lower than the overall poll in three of the next five general elections.

Percentage Polls

1938	79.4	1958	88.3
1943	75.3	1961	77.9
1948	78.9	1966	83.0
1953	85.0	1970	74.3

Nor was there a sense of great national crisis in 1948. This conclusion, admittedly impressionistic, is based upon interviews and a careful reading of the South African press throughout these years. N. J. Rhoodie and H. J. Venter contend otherwise but they provide little evidence. Moreover, these two authors concede that "despite the temporary delay caused by the War," there were "definite signs of a new Afrikaner solidarity" by 1945 when already "the majority of Afrikaners were decidedly Nationalists at heart."[40] Certainly, both official circles and private persons were troubled in 1948 by the wartime deterioration in domestic African affairs — witness the appointment in 1946 of the Native Laws Commission and the founding of the South African Bureau of Racial Affairs (SABRA) in 1947. Yet there is no known evidence of widespread *public* alarm regarding race relations. Clearly, there was no popular feeling comparable to the intense and even emotional enthusiasm for Hertzog that was general among Afrikaners immediately after the war vote of 1939.[41] South Africa's great national crisis influencing the 1948 election results occurred nine years earlier, on September 4, 1939. It was brought about by General Smuts, and its issue was not racial but South African nationalist.

Summary

Principles that possess consummatory significance for those holding them are not readily subject to compromise. In September 1939, faced with Great Britain's entry into war, South Africa could not postpone, or ignore a clash between two such principles — the indivisibility of the British Crown, and the paramount importance of South African national interests. One of these principles had, therefore, to fail of realization. The cost for South Africa of the Union's deciding "for war" in 1939 was nearly all of the electoral margin of safety that sheltered the experiment of Fusion in the middle of the 1930's. Ultimately, this cost, when coupled with a mild turn of the political tide against Smuts, meant the return of Afrikaner nationalists to power.

[40]N. J. Rhoodie and H. J. Venter, *Apartheid: A Socio-historical Exposition of the Origin and Development of the Apartheid Idea* (Cape Town: HAUM, 1959), p. 166.
[41]For a discussion, see Pirow, *James Barry Munnik Hertzog,* p. 250.

A little more than a decade after 1948, the triumph of nationalist parties in sub-Saharan Africa had become commonplace, as in the late 1950s and early 1960s in one country after another black men gained power to rule themselves. Of the political success of nationalist parties in tropical Africa, many if not most observers have approved, seeing in that success a potential for social integration, modernization, and the politicization (which some have taken to signify democratization) of previously dependent peoples. However, the political triumph in 1948 of Afrikaner nationalists, who in attitudes, aspirations, and behavior often resembled African nationalists, seemed to portend the social disintegration of the larger South African society and the antithesis of democracy, for to rule himself the Afrikaner had necessarily to rule others for whom he evidently did not feel equal responsibility. Because of this, his political triumph has commonly been regretted, save by the Afrikaner nationalist himself.

Was there a practical alternative to the domination of one group by another in South Africa? An affirmative answer to this question was the promise of Fusion, although that promise extended only to relations between the two white language groups, and not at all to non-whites. The "purified" Nationalists disagreed, of course. For them Fusion was a deception, disguising an unwitting acceptance by the Afrikaner of a society in which British traditions would be dominant. The importance of the war vote of September 4, 1939, was that it brought many other Afrikaners to this view. Thereafter, most Afrikaners believed that the choice in South African politics was between a British South Africa and an Afrikaner South Africa, and while they had the power to do so, it was clear they would choose the latter and feel, moreover, no moral delinquency in doing so. Certainly, Afrikaner nationalism was the foremost goal of the government elected in 1948. Eight of the twelve new ministers were former "purified" Nationalists, including, in addition to Malan himself, such leading anti-Fusionists as Strijdom, Swart, and Erasmus. After the general election of 1948, it seemed likely that the opportunity afforded in 1910, and again in 1934, for the development of a united South African white nation through the processes of compromise and conciliation had been lost, at least for the life of the new government, and that white unity, if it were to be achieved at all, would be founded on principles dictated by Afrikaners.

Looking backward, it seems possible to argue that the success of Fusion was of greater importance to both the Union and the British Commonwealth than was the need in 1939 for immediate South African action against Hitler, considering the necessarily limited role that was open to South Africa in this regard. From this standpoint, General Smuts — whose decision it was to press the issue — ought instead to have followed his life-long practice in politics and, as President Franklin Roosevelt did at the same time, have "let things develop" until a consensus for war could be found.

9.

Epilogue: 1948 to 1970

ALTHOUGH in retrospect the 1948 general election appears as a decisive turning point in South African politics, at the time and for some years thereafter it was by no means clear that the voting strength of the Alliance parties in 1948 would prove lasting and durable. Smuts, for one, told Hofmeyr at the end of June that he did not regard the election results as really decisive, although the situation was "damnably difficult."[1] It was thus not surprising that among the first measures taken by the new government in 1948 were several directed at ensuring that its parliamentary majority would not be at the mercy of small changes in public support.

It has been observed repeatedly in this work that the strength of the National Party up to 1948 was dependent on two factors: the proportion of the electorate who were Afrikaners, and Afrikaner political solidarity. Nationalist strategy obviously sought to increase both of these. While in opposition from 1934 to 1948, there was little that Nationalists could do to increase the Afrikaans-speaking proportion of the electorate, and during these years their energies were directed instead at promoting "national-mindedness" among Afrikaners and Afrikaner political unity. After 1948, however, the Nationalists were in a position to use their newly won power to protect and bolster the Afrikaner majority in the electorate. Indeed, one of Malan's first steps as premier was to curtail his predecessor's immigration program and to lengthen the residency requirement for naturalization of British subjects from two years to the usual five years. Then,

[1]Hancock, *Smuts, Vol. II,* p. 499.

in 1949 the Union's constitution was altered to allow parliamentary representation for whites living in South-West Africa. Significantly, 66 percent of the whites of South-West Africa were Afrikaners, and another 8 percent were German-speaking. The basis for the representation of South-West Africa in the House of Assembly was especially favorable; at the end of 1953 the average number of voters in the six constituencies in the Territory was less than half the number required everywhere else in the Union. Since the first elections in 1950, all MPs elected from South-West Africa have been Nationalists.

Also, in 1951 the government introduced legislation to eliminate Coloureds from the common voters' roll in the Cape, where they may have had considerable influence in perhaps half the number of seats,[2] and place them on a separate voter's roll to elect four whites to the House of Assembly. (In 1949 the right of Indians to elect two whites to the House of Assembly was ended, although that right had not been exercised in practice.) Nationalist leaders expected that the removal of the Coloureds would give them eight or nine extra seats in the Cape,[3] excluding the new Coloured seats, but constitutional issues impeded the progress of the legislation, and the Coloured were not removed from the common voters' roll until 1955.[4] The threat of removal, however, appears to have been behind the reduction by one-fifth in the number of Coloured voter registrations between 1951 and 1955.

The admission of six Nationalists from South-West Africa to the House of Assembly in 1950 may have been a critical development, for it relieved Malan of dependence on Havenga and the eight other Afrikaner Party MPs. There is little doubt that in the last half of 1948 tensions between Malan and Havenga nearly reached the breaking point on the issue of the former's plans for alteration of the non-white franchise.

[2]Carter, *The Politics of Inequality,* p. 122.
[3]R. R. Farguharson, "South Africa 1958," in D. E. Butler (ed.), *Elections Abroad* (London: Macmillan and Co., 1959), p. 232n.
[4]For an excellent account of this controversy, see Geoffrey Marshall, "South Africa: The Courts and the Constitution," in his *Parliamentary Sovereignty and the Commonwealth* (Oxford: Clarendon Press, 1957), pp. 139-248.

If Havenga had taken the Afrikaner Party out of the government and joined Smuts in 1948 or 1949, the Nationalists would have been out of power. Hancock writes that in November of 1948, the leadership of the United Party agreed "that informal soundings of Havenga's state of mind should be taken," but there is no evidence that discussions actually occurred.[5] Shortly thereafter, it was too late. Hancock states that "Smuts had missed his chance, if ever it existed, of preventing the Nationalists from digging in."[6] In 1951 the Afrikaner Party and the HNP merged to become the National Party, the NP.

But however important it may have been during the first few years of the new government, the 1953 elections showed there was more to the growing power of the National Party than just electoral entrenchment. Of the 156 seats that were filled, the Nationalists won 94, while the combined opposition was reduced to 62 seats. The Nationalists continued to receive fewer votes than their opponents, but the government's share of the total vote, including estimates for uncontested seats, was 45.5 percent, up 2.0 percent from 1948. Doubtless there were many factors contributing to this growth: the death within a period of eleven months of both Hofmeyr and Smuts; the single-mindedness and determination of the Nationalist administration; the race issue; and, conversely, the disunity of the opposition. Using Lord Balfour's useful distinction between "fundamentals" (those matters upon which there exists a broad public concensus) and "details" (those matters about which people do argue), it can be said that one cause of the Nationalists' success in 1953 was their ability to keep one of the South African fundamentals, that is, a belief in racial segregation, the principal political issue. Yet five years later at the general election of 1958, with the political context not greatly different from that in 1953, the Nationalists further increased their parliamentary representation to 103 seats and received 49.0 percent of the vote, including estimates for uncontested seats. And three years after this, at the general election of 1961, the Nationalists won 105 seats and

[5]Hancock, *Smuts, Vol. II,* p. 515.
[6]*Ibid.,* p. 516.

53.5 percent of the vote. The shootings at Sharpeville in March 1960, the racial disturbances and economic panic that followed, the May 1961 inauguration of the Republic, and South Africa's forced withdrawal from the British Commonwealth certainly created strong attitude forces influencing the vote in October of 1961.

Nevertheless, over the period of thirteen years between the general elections of 1948 and 1961, there can be little doubt that the growing strength of the National Party was less a consequence of momentary issues, or what Key terms "the artful strokes of skillful campaigners," than the product of long-term trends affecting a "secular realignment" in partisan attitudes.[7] (See Figure 3.) First, as we have indicated previously, among whites, birth rates favored Afrikaners. (In 1959 the electoral impact of this differential was advanced three years when the voting age was lowered from 21 years to 18 years, a move whose timing was certainly related to plans for holding a national referendum on the question of becoming a republic in 1960.)[8]

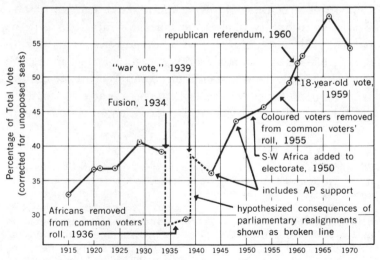

Figure 3. Secular growth in Nationalist electoral support, 1915-1970.

[7]V. O. Key, Jr., "Secular Realignment and the Party System," *Journal of Politics,* XXI, No. 2 (May 1959), 198-199.
[8]L. Longmore, "The Teenage Vote in South Africa," *Political Quarterly,* XXX, No. 2 (April-June 1959), 117.

Second, there was the cumulative impact on politics of the Afrikaner separatist movement that had begun in the 1930s and continued thereafter, often assisted by the power of the state after 1948. For example, Stanley Trapido notes that a foremost purpose of the Suppression of Communism Act of 1950 was to remove non-Nationalists from the leadership of the predominantly Afrikaans-speaking working class.[9] Finally — for growing Afrikaner nationalism was not the whole story — there was the emergence in the 1950s of race discrimination as a major world issue. In South Africa there were two consequences of this development. On the one hand, it aroused bitter criticism of South Africa overseas, but the effect of this may only have been to cause the electorate to unite behind the government's defense of the country's "peculiar institution." On the other hand, it undermined public confidence in the feasibility of the United Party's middle way between full racial integration and complete racial separation. Moreover, press reports of race atrocities in Kenya in the early 1950s, and later in Angola and the Republic of the Congo, and accounts of growing one-party rule in Nkrumah's Ghana were hardly likely to encourage whites to tread the path of political integration with the non-whites.

By 1958, these trends working together had made the Afrikaner Volk dominant and electorally secure in its own land. Its ultimate survival was no longer a matter of domestic electoral politics but, as R. R. Farguharson pointed out,

---

[9]Trapido, "Political Institutions and Afrikaner Social Structure," p. 82. Nationalist political power was also used to promote Afrikaner separatism in public education. In 1943 the Smuts government chose to fight the provincial council elections on the issue of support for dual-medium public education. (Public education of whites was the responsibility of the provincial administrations.) In 1943 Smuts failed in the Free State, but in the three other provinces he enjoyed a considerable triumph. The victory in the Transvaal, which was to give the 1948 general election to the Nationalists, might have been of considerable long-term political importance had the dual-medium policy been continued. However, in 1949, the Nationalists captured control of the Transvaal Provincial Council and soon abolished dual-medium education in favor of mother-tongue instruction.

"would depend on whether it could reach an accommodation with its own continent."[10]

A Politics of Security

In our study of the 1961 South African election, Jeffrey Butler and I suggested that despite the continuation of electoral trends favorable to the National Party that had been in evidence in six successive elections since 1938, it would be difficult for the Nationalists to increase their proportion of the total vote in the future.[11] Our reason for this suggestion was that the NP already had the support of nearly all Afrikaners, but as a party with strong identification with the Afrikaner Volk, it would be unable to develop significant support among non-Afrikaner voters. The 1966 election results showed that we had been mistaken. The Nationalists increased their percentage of the total vote from 53.5 percent to 58.6 percent, and in a House of Assembly that was larger by ten seats, the number of Nationalist MPs went up from 102 to 126. Although Denis Worrall has written that the 1966 Nationalist "gain among English-speaking voters was not as spectacular as had been anticipated," there could be no doubt that for the first time the National Party had appreciable English-speaking support.[12] A turning point in South African politics seemed to have arrived. Later I wrote that a "politics of security" characterized South Africa from 1961 until at least 1966, and that it was qualitatively different from South African politics before the creation of the Republic in 1961.[13] One aspect of this difference was the emergence of an official doctrine of white unity that is reminiscent of the older policy of conciliation, although with an important difference. Conciliation proposed white unity through the processes of compromise and accommodation; "neo-conciliation," as the new

[10]Farguharson, "South Africa 1958," p. 275.
[11]Newell M. Stultz and Jeffrey Butler, "The South African General Election of 1961," *Political Science Quarterly,* LXXVIII, No. 1 (March 1963), p. 86.
[12]Denis Worrall, "South Africa's 'Partition Election,' " *Africa Report,* XI, No. 5 (May 1966), p. 26.
[13]Newell M. Stultz, "The Politics of Security: South Africa under Verwoerd, 1961-6," *Journal of Modern African Studies,* VII, No. 1 (April 1969), pp. 3-20.

doctrine can be termed, proposed white unity through a process that is essentially one of assimilation, or absorption of English-speaking whites into the Afrikaner community. In slightly different presentation, this argument is repeated below.

The organizational framework for this argument is provided by David Apter, who has written that a "necessary object" of government is the preservation of its legitimacy, and that government responds to threats to this legitimacy by varying the relationship between its two reciprocal "functional requisites," information and coercion.[14] Variation in this relationship is in turn reflected in change in the structure of government, and justified — legitimized — by change in its values, that is, in official ideology.

New Challenge to Legitimacy

The legitimacy of government, according to Apter, has two aspects: the ultimate or end-values of government (the consummatory values of government); and the effectiveness of government. After 1948, two distinctive clusters of end-values supported the legitimacy of the government among the white South African electorate. One of these was associated with Afrikaner nationalism; the second had to do with white supremacy. For reasons discussed later, the importance of Afrikaner nationalism in South African politics commenced to decline with the establishment of the Republic in 1961. Nevertheless, the basic challenge from the parliamentary opposition continued to be an attack on the alleged commitment of the Nationalists to exclusive Afrikaner values. Domestic and international opposition to white supremacy also occurred, of course. Indeed, such opposition has a long history. Before 1960, however, opponents of race discrimination both within the country and outside it accepted the necessity of working *within* the governmental structures of the Union. That is, it was assumed that through the processes of education and persuasion, the white leaders of South Africa could be brought to a new conception of the purposes of their rule. Some persons and organizations continue in this view, but

[14]Apter, *The Politics of Modernization,* esp. 237-253.

about 1961 important elements opposing apartheid gave up the idea that South African whites can be persuaded to abandon race discrimination voluntarily. These elements now believe that the regime will change its policies only when it is *forced* to do so. In consequence, in the early 1960s there developed an unprecedented attack on the very *governing capacity* of the South African government.

The new challenge was most obvious in the international setting, especially at the United Nations, whose African membership grew from nine states in 1960 to 32 in October 1962. After 1961, South Africa was openly threatened at the U.N. with diplomatic and economic isolation, and even with military intervention; and in 1963 the newly created Organization of African Unity virtually declared war on all nonrepresentative regimes in southern Africa. In addition, after 1961 increasing numbers of states engaged in various gestures of opposition to South Africa, for example, supporting South Africa's exclusion from the Olympic Games. Largely symbolic, and of no consequence in themselves to the effectiveness of the government in South Africa, these gestures suggested a growing climate of international opinion that in the future might support stronger coercive action against the country.

Before 1952, protests within South Africa against race discrimination were, on the whole, both legal and orderly. In 1952 several groups adopted the tactic of passive resistance. This was, however, an appeal to the consciences of whites, not a threat to governmental effectiveness. But in 1960, in the wake of the widespread rioting that followed the Sharpeville shootings, the African National Congress and the Pan-Africanist Congress, the two largest non-white political organizations, were banned, and subsequently the already considerable police powers of the government were greatly expanded and vigorously applied to immobilize non-white and, to a lesser degree, white liberal political leaders. After 1961, the organization of public demonstrations of protest against race discrimination was extraordinarily difficult, and those that did occur were noteworthy for their spontaneous and anomic character. Instead of organizing public demonstrations, the non-white political organizations, most of which were now underground, and some whites turned in the early 1960s to acts of sabotage and a direct challenge to the effectiveness of the regime.

By the middle of the decade, this new challenge had scarcely taxed the resources of the state. Overseas threats had not resulted in meaningful penalties, while within the country sabotage had been of limited scope, with little loss of life. Still, reports of threats from overseas and of sabotage at home were circulated widely in the South African press, and a series of show trials highlighted for the public the existence of subterranean bodies following strategies of violence. For most whites, life continued as before. Many, however, discounted their comforts in the light of future possibilities, perceiving a long-term insecurity in their position.

Increasing Coercion

All governments are in some measure coercive. Moreover, non-whites in South Africa in particular have long lived in an environment of high governmental coercion. In the early 1960s, however, the level of official coercion in South Africa increased dramatically as a response of the government to the new challenge to its effectiveness. Especially significant (for this analysis) was the unprecedented application of arbitrary police power to large numbers of whites.

The coercive powers that were newly taken by the South African government are well known. They included the right to ban organizations, to restrict the activities of individuals (including house arrest), and to detain persons without charge. An indication of the extent to which these powers were applied was provided by a piece of National Party campaign literature at the time of the 1966 general election. This document, *Vrugte van die Nasionale Bewind, 1948-1966*, asserted that since 1960, 366 persons had been placed under house arrest or other restrictions, 356 had been prohibited from attending gatherings, and 294 had been ordered to report regularly to the police. In 1965 the Minister of Justice revealed that a total of 1,095 persons had been detained under the so-called 90-day clause, which had been suspended a short while before. Of this total, 102 had been whites, 40 of whom were subsequently charged with a specific offense.[15] In 1965 the police were authorized to detain state witnesses for up to six months and by August 1966, 125 such persons had been detained, 41 of whom were white.[16] Between 1960 and 1966 nearly 10,000 persons were detained or arrested for offenses or for reasons of a political character.[17] The size of the daily prison population is possibly a general indicator of the level of coercion. From 1957 to June 1965 this figure nearly doubled, from 38,920 to 76,227, although the total population of the country had increased by only one quarter.[18]

The opportunities open to the government for the coercion of foreign opponents of apartheid are, obviously, limited. Such opportunities as did exist were, however, exploited. Increasingly, entry visas were denied to persons thought to be even mildly critical of the regime, while domestic critics wishing to travel overseas experienced greater difficulty in obtaining passports. In 1962, 88 applications for passports were denied; in 1964 the number was 443.[19] Three dozen control posts were established in 1963 on the borders of the Republic, and transit visas are now required of persons wishing only to enter Lesotho. Occasionally requests for transit visas have been refused, even from nationals of Lesotho. Also in 1963 measures were introduced to control the flights of aircraft over South African territory into the three neighboring High Commission Territories. The General Laws Amendment Act of 1963 made it a capital offense for residents or former residents of the Republic to advocate, at any place outside the country, foreign intervention in South Africa.

Of greater consequence, the government worked to increase the cost or difficulty of implementing international sanctions against the Republic. Efforts were made to reduce the dependence of the country on imports, particularly on imports

[15]*House of Assembly Debates,* Vol. 13, January 29, 1965, cols. 252-267.
[16]*House of Assembly Debates,* Vol 17, August 1, 1966, cols. 18-19.
[17]Information Service of the National Party, *Vrugte van die Nasionale Bewind, 1948-1966,* p. 70.
[18]Muriel Horrell, *A Survey of Race Relations in South Africa: 1963* (Johannesburg: SAIRR, 1964), p. 312; House of Assembly Debates, Vol. 16, January 28, 1966, cols. 261-2.
[19]*House of Assembly Debates,* Vol. 14, April 30, 1965, cols. 5099-5100.

of oil, and in 1964 the government accepted the obligation
to spend $160 million over five years on the development
of South-West Africa. This was more than twice the level
of expenditure recommended in 1955 for the African reserve
areas of South Africa as a whole. An obligation to match
this investment would presumably devolve upon any governmental body that someday succeeds in replacing South Africa
as the administrator of South-West Africa.

Most obvious was the increasingly rapid development of
the South African Defence Force. In 1961/62 South Africa
spent $100 million on the Force; in 1966/67 the defense
budget had risen to $358 million and constituted 15.5 percent
of the total national budget.[20] Plans were announced in 1966
for one year of obligatory military service for all able-bodied
young white men.

Reduced Information

Coercion and information, Apter writes, are reciprocal
functions: the more coercion, the less information, and vice
versa. It is clear that as coercion increased in South Africa
in the early 1960s, it was accompanied by growing official
intolerance of political dissent, particularly of dissent on the
political left. In the 1950s, the boundary of "legitimate"
political opposition within the white electorate was approximately the line separating the communist left from the
non-communist left. In the 1960s, however, that boundary
moved towards the center, and by the end of the decade it
appeared to be the line separating the nonracial Liberal Party
from the Progressives. Many examples of decreasing information in South African politics might be cited, but three
illustrations seem particularly apt.

1. The Liberal Party did not contest any seat at the 1966
general election because most of its leading members and
organizers had been immoblized by banning orders. In the
election five years earlier, Liberals had contested two seats
as a means of presenting their views to the public. When
racially mixed political parties became illegal in 1968, the

[20]*House of Assembly Debates,* Vol. 17, August 24, 1966, col. 1381.

Liberal Party decided that its continued existence would be inconsistent with its nonracial philosophy and disbanded.

2. The resources of the government-controlled broadcasting monopoly, the South African Broadcasting Corporation (SABC), were increasingly employed in open attacks on institutions and bodies perceived as being hostile to the regime, including the English-language press, the Institute of Race Relations, the National Union of South African Students, the Defence and Aid Fund (banned in 1966), and the Christian Institute. Demands from these organizations for the right to reply to attacks by the SABC were usually refused. On 27 April 1964, the Leader of the Opposition charged that public funds were being used improperly to "propagate a political point of view."Responding, Prime Minister H. F. Verwoerd defended the right of the SABC "to guide the people to consider the interests of South Africa and South Africa only."[21]

3. In 1963, the government established a Publications Control Board with authority to ban publications, recordings, and films, and prohibit the performance of entertainments deemed "undesirable" by the Board. "Every week or so," stated the *Survey of Race Relations in South Africa* in 1966, "a further long list appears in the *Government Gazette* of publications that have been banned. . . . Some books have been prohibited recently for the apparent reason that they deal with inter-racial or political matters and contain conclusions that are not acceptable to right-wing opinion."[22]

Writing in 1965 on the absence of "feedback" in the making of South African foreign policy, Edwin Munger asserted that "the 'laager mentality,' as the English language press sometimes dubs it, is certainly enhanced by the sense of national peril, *while vigorous and radical debate is sacrificed*" (my italics).[23]

[21]*House of Assembly Debates,* Vol. 10, April 27, 1964, cols. 4957 and 5016.
[22]Horrell, *A Survey of Race Relations in South Africa: 1966, pp. 60-61.*
[23]Edwin Munger, *Notes on the Formation of South African Foreign Policy* (Pasadena: The Castle Press, 1965), p. 74.

Centralization of Decision-Making

The growing exercise of coercion by government in South Africa was accompanied by change in the relationship between Apter's two "structural requisites of government," decision-making and accountability. Specifically, decision-making became increasingly centralized, as the influence of interest groups was reduced.

There are many examples of these developments. Mention has previously been made of the banning in 1960 of the African National Congress and the Pan-Africanist Congress, and of the official pressure that was subsequently brought to bear upon such organizations as the Liberal Party, the Institute of Race Relations, and the National Union of South African Students. Similarly, there was a noticeable intensification of and intimidate the English-language press, certain church groups, such as the ecumenical Christian Institute, and the English-medium South African universities. "Detention-without-trial" laws and the banning of the Defence and Aid efforts by the government and its sympathizers to discredit Fund can be seen as efforts at freeing the administration of justice from the encumbrance of an independent judiciary.

Subsystem autonomy, never a pronounced feature of contemporary South Africa, was further reduced after 1961. Three examples may suffice. Following an altercation in 1965 between the University of Cape Town and the Minister of Education, Arts, and Science concerning the right of the University to debar a student organization restricting its membership on racial grounds, the government published the University Amendment Bill. This measure would have made it illegal for a university administration to prohibit race discrimination on its campus; it was withdrawn when the University of Cape Town capitulated and agreed not to do so. In March 1967, Parliament passed the National Education Policy Bill, which transfers control of the education of whites from the provincial administrations to the central government. Finally, in 1967 the government obtained authority from Parliament to compel the decentralization of private industry to the borders of the African areas. Other sectors in South African life were commonly no less free of govern-

ment intervention than the universities, provincial administrations, and private industry.

Edwin Munger wrote in 1965 that "the South African
Government has traditionally been opposed to pressure
groups and resistant to them," but that Prime Minister
Verwoerd had a "particular anathema to organized pressure."
In fact, Munger dismissed the influence of nearly all groups
in the making of South African foreign policy, and suggested,
"If one were to list the most important people making foreign
policy, the names might well run: (1) Dr. Verwoerd; (2) Dr.
Verwoerd; (3) Dr. Verwoerd."[24]

Particularly relevant were indications of the absence of
"consent groups" within the National Party and the Afrikaner
"establishment."[25] J. D. du P. Basson, who was at the time
a Nationalist MP, has asserted that Dr. Verwoerd introduced
the Promotion of Bantu Self-Government Bill in Parliament
in 1959 without prior consultations with senior bodies of the
party or even the parliamentary caucus,[26] and my attention
has been drawn to the fact that at no time did Verwoerd
allow public discussion of the government's "Bantustan"
program at National Party congresses. The so-called 'great
purge' of the independent-minded leadership of the South
African Bureau of Racial Affairs in 1961 is an especially telling
illustration of the concentration of decision-making power
in South Africa under Verwoerd. Writing of this episode, J.
F. Holleman, who was present as an external observer, noted:
"It is natural, and indeed necessary, to view the removal of
Sabra's independent spirits with deep apprehension and anxiety, for [it] can but serve as a cynical reminder that the
pursuit of scientific investigation and the presentation of
scientific truth in this country is in danger of becoming a
privilege requiring political negotiation and governmental
sanction."[27]

[24]*Ibid.*, pp. 85 and 100.
[25]Apter defines a "consent group" as a body from which assent to
a decision is required by law or practice before it becomes binding
(*The Politics of Modernization,* p. 247).
[26]Gwendolen M. Carter, Thomas Karis, and Newell M. Stultz, *South
Africa's Transkei: The Politics of Domestic Colonialism* (Evanston:
Northwestern University Press, 1967), p. 52.
[27]J. F. Holleman, "S.A.B.R.A. 1961: The Great Purge," a report

Changing Ideology

As Apter's analysis would cause one to anticipate, the increased exercise of coercion by government in South African life was accompanied by a manipulation of the values of white politics to legitimize that coercion and maintain social solidarity among whites. The new values can perhaps be aptly summarized in the following statement of the overriding purpose of the Republican government in the middle of the 1960s: *preservation of white South Africa from the forces of communism through white unity.* Earlier, as I have tried to show, the purpose of the rule of the National Party was more narrow: preservation of Afrikanerdom from the domination of non-Afrikaner influences through Afrikaner unity. The value substitutions were thus: (1) white nationalism for Afrikaner nationalism; (2) white unity for Afrikaner unity; and (3) anti-communism for Afrikaner ethnocentrism.

1. White Nationalism. The last South African election at which it could be realistically supposed that the National Party could be removed from power was probably that which occurred in 1953. Certainly, after the 1958 election few could doubt that, in the absence of a split within the party, Nationalists were to be in office for a very long time. Nationalist political dominance was, however, in part a consequence of the South African electoral system which, as we have seen, gives greater weight to the votes of those in rural areas than it does to the votes of city dwellers. Even in 1958, although the National Party captured 103 of 163 seats in the House of Assembly, the NP did not receive a majority of the popular vote, if allowance is made for uncontested seats.

But the foremost objective of the National Party after 1948, demonstrated in Dr. Verwoerd's first speech to the country upon becoming premier in September 1958, was the transformation of South Africa into a republic,[28] and it will be recalled that as early as the 1940s, the principle had been accepted by the Nationalists that such a transformation would require the concurrence of a majority of the electorate, voting at

---

to the Institute for Social Research, University of Natal, prepared by its director (Durban, 1961), mimeo, p. 17.

[28]*Africa Digest,* VI, No. 2 (September-October 1958), 56.

a special public referendum, all votes counting equally. Thus as late as 1958 it was not at all certain that Afrikanerdom was sufficiently united to ensure the creation of a republic in South Africa, and accordingly Afrikaner leaders persisted long after the National Party was safely entrenched in stressing the importance of Afrikaner group identity and solidarity and trying to isolate Afrikaners from influences that might reduce this group self-confidence.

The republican objective was realized in October 1960 when at a public refendum 52.3 percent of the white electorate supported the abolition of the Monarchy. (Coloured voters were not entitled to vote.) United Afrikanerdom had met the test, and the need for Afrikaner unity immediately lessened. Concurrently, government leaders perceived a need to justify higher levels of official coercion to defend their rule and chose to do so on the grounds of self-defense of the white nation.

It would be an error to dismiss Afrikaner nationalism as a potent force in current South African affairs; but whereas a narrow ethnic appeal was once the stock in trade of Nationalist politicians, after 1960 such an appeal was considered inappropriate. The first sentence of the National Party's 1958 election manifesto read, "The National Party stands for South Africa First" — an allusion to the alleged divided loyalty of English-speaking South Africans. But speaking to the Transvaal congress of the National Party only three years later, Prime Minister Verwoerd could say, "I see the National Party *today* ... as a party which stands for the preservation of the white man, of a White government in South Africa" (my italics).[29] Muriel Horrell's 1963 *Survey of Race Relations* observed that "White right-wing elements (English — as well as Afrikaans-speaking people) are increasingly aligning themselves behind Dr. Verwoerd, who is coming to be looked upon by them as the champion of *White* nationalism rather than of *Afrikaner* nationalism, as in the past."[30]

Certain structural changes in administration reflected this

[29]*Rand Daily Mail,* August 17, 1961.
[30]Horrell, *A Survey of Race Relations in South Africa: 1963,* p. 1.

change in values. In 1961 the government established a department of immigration to encourage the immigration of whites to the Republic. Thirteen years earlier, it will be recalled, the Nationalists under Dr. Malan had, upon assuming office, curtailed the post-war immigration program begun by General Smuts. Malan had feared that large-scale immigration would reduce the power of Afrikaner nationalism. As head of the new department, Verwoerd appointed an English-speaking conservative, A. E. Trollip, and, concurrently, another English-speaker was appointed Minister of Information and Tourism. Between 1948 and 1961, only Afrikaners had been in the cabinet. Six Nationalist candidates in the general election of 1966 were English-speaking. This, too, had no precedent.

2. White Unity. Prior to 1960, as we have said, Afrikaner nationalists had been primarily concerned with maintaining the political unity of all Afrikaners, and one tactic that had been adopted was an effort to reduce the number of cross-pressures to which Afrikaners might be subject as a result of their membership with non-Afrikaners in various voluntary associations. After 1960, however, the government appeared to be more tolerant of the development of cross-pressures that could weaken the solidarity of Afrikaners, if concurrently these cross-pressures could be seen to strengthen white unity. In 1964, for example, the government provided for the establishment of a dual-medium (English and Afrikaans) university at Port Elizabeth.

On the other hand, it is even more important that the government exploited its authority and power to eliminate as far as possible any associational contact between whites and non-whites. At the end of 1962 professional and scientific bodies receiving government subsidies were threatened with the loss of those subsidies if they did not exclude non-whites from their membership.[31] The Prohibition of Improper Interference Bill, introduced in 1966, would have made it an offense for a person of one race to be a member of or take part in the activities of an organization of "another racial group" that had as its purpose the propagation, discussion, study,

[31]*House of Assembly Debates,* Vol. 5, March 5, 1963, cols. 2140-2141.

or encouragement of "political views." Because of widespread opposition to the measure, the bill was referred to a select committee of Parliament before the second reading, but it was reintroduced and passed in 1968. Even so, by 1966 a situation had already been reached in which, between whites and non-whites, nearly all cleavages were constant, and as a result the focus of social conflict and social ideas increasingly shifted upwards to the level of the racial communities themselves.

3. Anti-communism. While Afrikaner unity remained a prime tactical objective of Nationalist rule, Afrikaner nationalism, resting on the distinctive history, language, and culture of the Afrikaner people, provided an effective, mobilizing ideology. The new emphasis on white unity, however, makes Afrikaner nationalism obsolete; its social referents are too narrow. But a substitute doctrine that could bind together all whites in South Africa has been difficult to construct, for except for skin color and a position of economic and political privilege as compared to non-whites, there is little that whites in South Africa share uniquely in common. Culturally, white South Africa is a fragmented community, and historical memories serve more to divide than to unite. On what principles should the white "nation" of South Africa unite? An answer to this problem was found in anti-communism. Of course, anti-communism was not new in South Africa. As early as 1950 Parliament passed the Suppression of Communism Act, outlawing the South African Communist Party. After 1960, however, anti-communism became a national (that is, a white) phobia, replacing the Anglophobia that was present in the thinking of many Afrikaner nationalists in earlier years.

An examination of the annual addresses at the State opening of Parliament, delivered by the Governor-General from 1958 to 1961, and by the State President from 1962 to 1966, provides an indication of this increased concern. In 1958, 1959, and 1960 there was no mention of communism, but each year thereafter the President drew the attention of the country to the alleged threat of communism to South Africa, and in 1962 nearly one-fifth of the President's address was given over to consideration of this subject.

These references reveal the utility of the issue of anti-communism to the government. International pressures upon South Africa were interpreted as an outgrowth of the communist effort at world domination. The objective of these pressures was seen not as the elimination of race discrimination but as the destruction of the Western influence in Africa as represented by the Republic. The complicity of Western countries in these pressures was explained as the misguided attempts of these countries to win the support of the new nations of Asia and Africa for purposes of the Cold War. Similarly, subversion within South Africa was seen as but the domestic extension of an international communist conspiracy. Thus attacks upon South Africa from abroad and sabotage at home were viewed not as the inevitable products of an inequitable social structure, but as the consequences of the present state of world politics, for which, obviously, the Republic could not be held responsible.

The government was not alone in sanctioning anti-communism. In April 1964, 2,000 whites, very many of whom were clergymen, gathered in Pretoria to attend a privately organized Volkskongres (People's Congress) on the theme "Christianity against Communism." In the past, the holding of a Volkskongres had been a periodic feature of Afrikaner nationalist politics. In 1934 a Volkskongres was convened to consider the "poor-white" problem. The economic position of Afrikaners was examined in 1939 and again in 1950. In 1944 the topic was South Africa's race policy. In every case, the convening of a Volkskongres marked the emergence of a new issue in Afrikaner politics and the beginning of a general effort at mobilizing the Afrikaner public. There is no doubt that Afrikaner nationalists controlled the 1964 meeting. It was estimated, however, that one-fifth of those attending were English-speaking, and it seems clear that the object of the Volkskongres was to alert all whites, not just Afrikaners, to the alleged perils of communist subversion in South Africa.

The 1964 Volkskongres established a continuing body, the National Council Against Communism. In 1966 the National Council sponsored an "International Symposium on Communism," held in Pretoria. Government support for the symposium is suggested by the fact that its chairman was the Reverend J. D. Vorster, brother of the next prime minister. The main speaker was Major Edgar Bundy, executive secretary of the Anti-Communist Church League of America. Bundy's role and the structuring of the symposium as an 'international' undertaking highlight the passing of narrow Afrikaner nationalist appeals in South African white politics.

The problem of constructing a national ethos for white South Africa is manifested in the identification of appropriate symbols, for historically symbols in South Africa have divided whites rather than united them. In the past, as we have seen, questions of the national flag and anthem sparked bitter political controversies. After 1960 the attempt was made to make the Republic itself a unifying symbol which might join all whites together. Government-sponsored celebrations in Pretoria marking the fifth anniversary of the Republic, which included an unprecedented display of the country's Defence Force, were on a scale seldom matched in South Africa. Yet, however meaningful it was to many Afrikaners, the republican constitutional form at first was little cherished by English-speaking whites, most of whom voted against the creation of the Republic in 1960.

It appears, rather, that by the time of his death in 1966 Verwoerd himself had become the most obvious symbol of white South Africa. Specifically, he had become a tangible manifestation of the unalterable will of whites to survive as a distinctive and independent political community. In November 1960 Verwoerd told Nationalists on the Witwatersrand that they would have to stand "like walls of granite" on their race policy because the very existence of the nation was at stake,[32] and subsequently a prominent feature of the Prime Minister's public image was his alleged rock-like inflexibility. A satire on South African politics written in 1963 referred to the Prime Minister as "Father Granite."[33] After Verwoerd's death, tributes to his leadership from different

[32]*The Star,* December 1, 1960.
[33]Anthony Delius, *The Day Natal Took Off* (Cape Town: Insight, 1963).

sections unanimously honored him for his steadfastness of purpose, indomitable spirit, and utter dedication.[34]

Among Afrikaner nationalists, past leaders of the National Party — Hertzog, Malan, and (although to a lesser extent) Strijdom — were in their day regarded as heroes. Indeed, recalling the Voortrekker leaders of the nineteenth century, it seems possible to suggest that personalized political authority is a feature of Afrikaner political culture. It was thus not surprising that Verwoerd was similarly canonized by Afrikaners, particularly after the realization of the republican ideal in 1961. The extension of the "charisma" of a Nationalist leader into the English-speaking community was, however, unprecedented. Yet during the general election of 1966, a tour by the Prime Minister through Natal, the most English of South African provinces, evoked scenes of public adoration and enthusiasm and contributed, later, to an electoral swing towards the National Party in that province of 14.4 percent. Evidently the "neo-conciliation" of Verwoerd that emerged during the last years of his premiership met its positive response in the English-speaking electorate.

Verkrampte Reaction

The new ideology just described proposes an end to the political isolation of Afrikaners that has been central to the orthodoxy of Afrikaner nationalism since at least the time of General Hertzog's articulation of the "two-stream" concept in 1912, if not from the time of President Paul Kruger before that. Inevitably, therefore, there are those Afrikaners who, much as Dr. Malan and other "purified" Nationalists in 1934 did, view the ending of this isolation as wrong. While Verwoerd lived, the force of his personality muted the division of opinion within the ranks of the government on this issue, although shortly before his death it was referred to publicly in the pages of *Die Burger*. After Verwoerd's assassination, however, the dissent intensified until in 1969 a minority were forced to leave the party.

[34]See, for example, Laurence Gandar's front-page editorial in the *Rand Daily Mail,* September 7, 1966.

In 1966, Professor W. J. de Klerk of Potchefstroom University used the Afrikaans word *verkrampte* ("cramped") to describe the arch-conservative wing of Afrikaner nationalism, and *verligte* ("enlightened") to refer to those who supported the innovate policies of Dr. Verwoerd, and comparative liberals in the government, and in a short while these terms were in general use.[35] Because of his earlier association with the Ossewa-Brandwag, and the vigor of his campaign against saboteurs and terrorists as Verwoerd's last Minister of Justice, the election of John Vorster as Verwoerd's successor in 1966 was widely viewed as a victory for the *verkrampte* wing of the government. But by the end of his first year in office, there was little doubt that the pragmatism of the new Prime Minister had led him into the *verligte* camp; increasingly thereafter Vorster was criticized by *verkrampte* dissidents within Afrikanerdom for allegedly having abandoned traditional Nationalist principles. Though the leading *verkrampte* was clearly 70 year old Dr. Albert Hertzog, the Minister of Health and Posts and Telegraph (and son of the country's third prime minister), the strength of the *verkramptes* appeared not to be in Parliament but in the leadership of various "national-minded" voluntary associations. Indeed, on July 27, 1967, the *Sunday Times* reported that *verkrampte* opinion had "infiltrated" all Afrikaner political and cultural bodies and was already dominant in a number of them.

In addition to objecting to the idea of further English-Afrikaner *rapprochement,* the *verkramptes* disputed the wisdom of the Prime Minister's policies in the fields of international sport, immigration, and foreign relations. In particular, the *verkramptes* opposed allowing foreign sporting teams to enter the Republic if they included non-white members; opposed large-scale immigration into South Africa, especially of swarthy and Roman Catholic southern Europeans; and opposed the exchange of diplomats with Malawi and other black African states.

[35]Patrick O'Meara, "Tensions in the Nationalist Party," *Africa Report,* XIV, No. 2 (February, 1969), 43.

But it was the principle of closer unity among Afrikaners and English-speaking whites, and increased membership of the latter in the National Party, that was the most important issue because of its direct challenge to the fundamental *verkrampte* belief that the strength of Afrikanerdom, and the salvation of South Africa, lay in the political isolation of Afrikaners. On April 14, 1969, in a speech in the House of Assembly, Dr. Albert Hertzog put this point of view as follows: Despite the fact that Afrikaners and English-speaking whites have much in common, there are important differences. Among these differences, there is the fact that Afrikaners are Calvinist, and because of this they do not hesitate to "maintain authority," so long as it is "just." The Afrikaner nationalist is thus an "ideal soldier" for white civilization. On the other hand, an ingrained liberalism is characteristic of most English-speaking persons, and because of this liberalism, they find it difficult to take action against those movements that attack them. Thus if white civilization is to survive in South Africa, Hertzog concluded, it is necessary that the Afrikaner's "spiritual make-up" be protected. And though he did not say so then, Hertzog left the impression that such protection required the political self-sufficiency (isolation) of the Afrikaner.[36] Six months later, Dr. A. P. Treurnicht, the editor of *Hoofstad,* the unofficial mouthpiece of the *verkramptes,* made the point explicit: "To the extent that more English-speaking people accept the political viewpoint of the Afrikaner and act with him in one political party, it is obvious that the party will no longer be able to look after the cultural interests of the Afrikaner [when they are in competition with those of the English culture]."[37]

The split in the National Party resulting from the *verkrampte-verligte* dissidence emerged slowly. In August 1967 Vorster for the first time acknowledged in public the existence of the *verkramptes* and said their views were inappropriate to current realities. Six months later, one of Hert-. zog's two cabinet portfolios was taken from him, and in

[36]*House of Assembly Debates,* April 14, 1969, cols. 3876-3883.
[37]*Rand Daily Mail,* October 11, 1969.

August of 1968 he was dropped from the cabinet altogether. Then responding to Hertzog's speech in the House of Assembly that has been summarized above, the Prime Minister declared on April 22, 1969, that Hertzog's views did not represent the standpoint of the government; and a few moments later, B. J. Schoeman, the Minister of Transport, declared: "I, as the Leader of the National Party in Transvaal, of which the hon. member for Ermelo [that is, Hertzog] is a member, unconditionally reject the allegations he made against English-speaking South Africans."[38]

Finally, in September the party leadership maneuvered for a showdown at the Transvaal congress of the National Party in Pretoria by introducing resolutions affirming government policy in each of the areas contested by the *verkramptes.* Hertzog and his Transvaal supporters accepted the challenge on the question of the government's sports policy, and when they were defeated, party practice required that they publicly affirm that policy, resign from the party, or be expelled. In time, Hertzog chose expulsion, upon which event one of his leading supporters observed, "Men like Dr. Hertzog ... have been kicked out [of the party] so that Maoris can play rugby in South Africa and for the sake of English-speaking people."[39] Twenty-nine years after General Hertzog exiled himself from the Free State National Party in defense of what C. R. Swart termed "the rights of the English," the party exiled the General's son to emphasize its affirmation of those rights.[40] Thereafter, Hertzog and three other MPs who followed him set about organizing a new party, which they named the Herstigte Nasionale Party (the Reconstituted National Party), the HNP. In both its spirit and its promise, the new party clearly desired to be likened to the "purified" National Party formed in 1934.

[38]*House of Assembly Debates,* Vol. 26, April 22, 1969, cols. 4506 and 4515.
[39]Mr. J. A. Marais, MP, quoted in the *Rand Daily Mail,* October 7, 1969.
[40]There was no irony in this event, for even while his father was United Party prime minister, Albert Hertzog's lack of enthusiasm for political cooperation of Afrikaners with English-speaking persons was well known.

But in 1934 General Hertzog did not respond to the defection of the "purified" Nationalists by dissolving Parliament. Dr. Malan and his followers thus continued to have the House of Assembly as a national platform for four years while they prepared for their first test of public support. In 1969 Prime Minister Vorster, possibly less confident than General Hertzog 35 years earlier, declined to give the "Herstigtes" any such period of grace. On September 17 he announced that a general election would be held on April 22, 1970, more than a year ahead of schedule. Indeed, during the ensuing campaign, although other parties and issues naturally intruded, the contest between the NP and the HNP for the right to represent the soul of Afrikanerdom was at the center of the public's interest, in part at least because of the novelty (in this generation) of Nationalists fighting among themselves in public. Inevitably, given the consummatory character of the issues that were involved, this struggle was a bitter exercise — all the more so when the government used its extraordinary security powers to harrass its HNP opponents. This application of power seemed to indicate the habits of political authority in contemporary South Africa as much as it did the government's perception of the threat presented by the HNP; for although the HNP entered candidates in 79 constituencies, few commentators gave it a chance to win more than three or four of these seats. The results of the voting on April 22 showed that even this estimate exaggerated the strength of the HNP. No HNP candidate was elected, and all but four lost their electoral deposits, including Hertzog himself at Ermelo which he had represented since 1948. The HNP's total of 53,763 votes was only 3.6 percent of all votes. Hertzog later excused this poor performance as an inevitable consequence of his party's newness and limited organization,[41] but a more compelling explanation is that the dominance of Afrikaner values in contemporary South Africa has eliminated the sense of comparative social deprivation among Afrikaners that provided the stimulus for Afrikaner nationalism in the past.

[41]*The Star,* April 24, 1970.

Meanwhile, the National Party polled 54.4 percent of the vote, down 4.2 percent from 1966, and lost nine seats — all to the United Party. More than half of the reduction in the government's share of the total vote, although none of its losses of seats, was due to the appearance of the HNP, but the government also lost support on a broad front to the United Party, ending 22 years of steady electoral decline on the part of the official parliamentary opposition. Government losses to the United Party were greatest in Natal and along Witwatersrand, giving credence to the contention of the political correspondent for *The Star* on April 23 that the government's "almost frantic" efforts to defend its right flank against the HNP had cost it much of its English-speaking support and returned partisan alignments to the pattern that had existed at the 1961 election. At the same time, the low turnout — 74.4 percent — suggested that, as in 1943, some Afrikaners may have responded to division in the Nationalist ranks by abstaining from voting. The full returns, by number of seats, were as follows:

1970 Election Results

National Party	117
United Party	47
Progressive Party	1
Reconstituted Nationalists	0
Vacant	1

The day after the election, Prime Minister Vorster said in Pretoria that he interpreted the election results as a "definite mandate" to continue past policies of the government, especially in the fields of race relations and "nation-building" between the two white language groups.[42] It is hard to see how a majority of 69 seats in a House of 166 members could not, in the context of the South African electoral system, be regarded as a mandate. Nevertheless, four years after the death of Dr. Verwoerd, the government's mobilizing power among both Afrikaners and English-speaking persons had been set back slightly, while, concurrently, sizable gains

[42]*Rand Daily Mail,* April 24, 1970.

by Progressive candidates at the expense of the United Party
suggested a movement of some voters to the left on matters
of race policy. An editorial in the *Rand Daily Mail* (April
23) spoke of a "thaw" in South African politics, and with
this conclusion most observers seemed able to agree. But if
South African public affairs in 1970 lacked the stultifying
rigidity of Verwoerd's latter years, the change was not yet
fundamental; for those general features which we identified
as characteristic of white politics during much of the Republic's first decade continued: high coercion and low information, a heirarchial political structure, and an official ideology
stressing group cohesion and group security.

The Future

Modernizing political systems that have the characteristics
just enumerated are termed by David Apter "mobilization
systems." Such systems, he states, when they are endowed
with elaborate technology and managerial staff, can move
towards greater totalitarianism.[43] Indeed, what I have termed
a "politics of security" in South Africa, others have seen as
growing totalitarianism. But "mobilization systems," Apter
believes, are likely to be short-lived: low levels of information
result in uncertainty in decision-making, political capri-
ciousness, and inefficiency in the realization of the material
goals of the polity. And when this inefficiency is prolonged,
it leads to political cynicism, a decline in "political religion,"
that is, in ideology, and a loss of legitimacy by government.[44]
In time, the system will necessarily change to another type
with different normative and/or structural characteristics.
Apter thus sees incompatibilities between the postulated
material ends of politics and the instrumental capabilities
of government as a prime source of political dynamics at the
level of the system itself.

Yet by the end of the decade of the 1960s, it was clear
that from the standpoint of the whites, at least, the South
African political system had not suffered loss of support by
reason of what David Easton calls "output failure." Nor was

[43]Apter, *The Politics of Modernization,* p. 388.
[44]*Ibid.*

there reason to believe that this was likely to occur in the foreseeable future in the absence of international intervention in the affairs of the Republic or a widespread uprising of non-whites within the country. In part the success of the South African regime was due to the fact that unlike the "mobilization system," that according to Apter is established to achieve rapid social *change*,[45] the South African "politics of security" was instituted to maintain and protect a social order, rather than to create one, and this is a considerably easier task. Still, even in developmental terms, South Africa was highly successful. Despite the concentration and central-ization of decision-making power under Verwoerd, the ma-chinery of government was not, on the whole, inefficient, as Julius Lewin has observed.[46] Moreover, while the Progressive Party has undoubtedly been correct when it has asserted that government policies are an encumbrance upon the economic welfare of the country, South Africa in the 1960s was materi-ally prosperous, indeed, strikingly so. Where ideology and economics did pull in different directions, as in the case of "job reservation," economics often prevailed. In 1966 Leonard Thompson wrote that the Republic's economy "is a strong economy by any standard and it is becoming stronger."[47]

But "output failure" is not the only kind of threat to the persistence of a "mobilization system;" obvious success in realizing its material goals may also produce political cyni-cism, Apter suggests, although such success is uncommon. Material prosperity increases secularization thus weakening ideology, and once the "revolution has been consolidated, its revolutionary achievements become remote to the next gen-eration."[48] Similarly, William Foltz has noted that "defending a revolution is always a less exciting and more onerous task than making it."[49]

[45]*Ibid.*, p. 40.
[46]Julius Lewin, *Politics and Law in South Africa* (London: Merlin Press, 1963), p. 110.
[47]Leonard M. Thompson, *Politics in the Republic of South Africa* (Boston: Little, Brown, 1966), p. 46.
[48]Apter, *The Politics of Modernization,* p. 306.
[49]Karl W. Deutsch and William J. Foltz (eds.), *Nation-Building* (New York: Atherton Press, 1966), p. 122.

In the middle of the 1960s a survey of urban Afrikaners revealed a surprisingly low level of concern with the values of Afrikaner nationalism. More than one-third had never attended a *volksfees* (a *volk*-celebration); half approved of dual-medium education for Afrikaans-speaking youth; and fewer than half wished to be called "Afrikaners" or "Afrikaans South Africans." Patrick O'Meara has interpreted these findings as showing the adverse consequences of urbanization and industrialization on Afrikaner group solidarity, and although comparative figures for rural Afrikaners are lacking, there can be little doubt that Afrikaner urbanization — seen both as a process of occupational and economic differentiation and cultural secularization — has had this effect.[50]

Yet as I have suggested earlier, another cause for the weakening of Afrikaner nationalism must also be the success of the National Party in the past in entrenching Afrikaner values, often in a dominant position, in South African national life, causing new generations of Afrikaners to take these values for granted. Were white South Africans to become similarly complacent about their security interests, would this lessen the impluse toward white unity, and rather than moving the county back to the dominance of Afrikaner nationalism, move it instead to a form of white polyarchy?

In some degree, such complacency had already appeared by 1970 and was one of the factors that lay behind the improved showing of both the United Party and the Progressive in the 1970 election. Although the success of the government's campaign against sabotage rings and terrorist organizations in the years 1960-1965 was apparent at the time of the 1966 election (on March 20, 1965, Vorster had boasted: "I gave the assurance that I would eradicate communist subversion in South Africa and that has been done"),[51] it seems likely that the initial public response to this success was increased support for the government, and that only later did the electorate begin to take domestic peace for granted. South Africa's economic prosperity and even such happenings

[50]O'Meara, "Tensions in the Nationalist Party," 24.
[51]Jan Botha, *Verwoerd Is Dead* (Cape Town: Books of Africa, 1967), p. 194.

as Dr. Christiaan Barnard's heart transplants gave further reassurance. But no less important than a dynamic economy and a competent security police were the tribulations of others abroad who presumed to judge the Republic: the refusal in July 1966 by the International Court of Justice to rule in the case brought by Ethopia and Liberia against South Africa's administration of South West Africa; the continuing inability of Great Britain to end Rhodesian succession; military coups, civil war, and economic stagnation among many of Africa's newly independent black states; the closing of the Suez Canal; the agony of America both at home and in Vietnam; Russia's confrontation with Communist China; and so forth. These and other similar examples of incapacity, violence, crisis, and confusion in the affairs of South Africa's critics provided not only moral, but also political reassurance. C. W. de Kiewiet wrote in February 1969: "The South African government is at a peak of confidence and self-assurance. It faces its critics and opponents with a level eye. It has the income to back bold decisions. It feels that the movement of events throughout the world has been predominantly in its favor, and continues to be so. Its supporters, who grow in each election, breathe easily. The prevailing state of mind can no longer be called a laager mentality made grimly solid by a sense of approaching doom. The country is visibly relaxed."[52]

But in de Kiewiet's view, this relaxation may prove to be only "a brief Indian summer before the harsh winds [of world unpopularity] blow again," and I have previously written that in the context of domestic and international threats against South Africa, security is not a terminal condition that, once achieved, can be forgotten. It is, rather, an ongoing need, for the "enemy" — communism, liberalism, the Afro-Asian states, and the United Nations — can be thwarted but not defeated. In the long run, the pressures experienced by the Republic in the early 1960s would seem certain to rise again, and intensify. If this be so, few whites should be vulnerable to growing complacency or cynicism regarding the security-

[52]C. W. de Kiewiet, "The World and Pretoria," *Africa Report,* XIV, No. 2 (February, 1969), 48.

oriented values of the regime. In sum, stimulated by a long-term if thus far unavailing challenge to the effectiveness of the regime, and being conservative rather than revolutionary in its purposes, the South African "politics of security" had not to 1970 exhibited the internal contradictions that Apter believes are characteristic of the "mobilization system" to which otherwise it bore a likeness. Nor was there reason to suppose it soon would. The persistence of this political form in South Africa, including a new emphasis on cooperative political relations between Afrikaners and English-speaking whites, thus appeared likely. In 1939, the pressures of world events acting on the Union had the effect of destroying the basis for large-scale political cooperation between the two white language groups. Three decades later, different external pressures were having the effect of reestablishing that cooperation.

Selected Bibliography

South Africa is without doubt the most thoroughly studied country in Africa; there exists an enormous literature, although an inordinate amount of this attention is recent. It should be noted, however, that most studies of South Africa are book length. The periodical literature on South Africa is surprisingly meager, although it too has increased markedly during the past decade. The following are works devoted primarily to white politics. The list of books, moreover, is limited to those that have been most useful in the present study; it is thus only suggestive. In particular, very many biographies and autobiographies have been omitted. Readers who desire a more complete listing, or fuller treatments of other topics — for example, race relations — are encouraged to consult any of the very extensive bibliographies provided by Gwendolen Carter, Thomas Karis, William Vatcher, and Heribert Adam at the end of their respective books cited below. Works in Afrikaans have been omitted here, but many Afrikaans titles appear in the footnotes.

Official Publications

Verbatim reports of parliamentary debates are bound annually for each House. The weekly *Government Gazette* is the official source for election returns, but does not indicate the party affiliations of the candidates. The *Official Yearbooks* (annual to 1960) hold much statistical information. Many valuable studies are found in the reports of various government commissions. An official guide is:

————. *Notes on the Formation of South African Foreign Policy.* Pasadena: The Castle Press, 1965.

Paton, Alan. *Hofmeyr.* Cape Town: Oxford University Press, 1964.

Patterson, Shelia. *The Last Trek: A Study of the Boer People and the Afrikaner Nation.* London: Routledge & Kegan Paul, 1957.

Roberts, Michael, and A. E. G. Trollip, *The South African Opposition, 1939-1945: An Essay in Contemporary History.* Cape Town: Longmans, Green, 1947.

Simons, H. J., and Simons, R. E. *Class and Colour in South Africa, 1850-1950.* Baltimore: Penguin Books, 1969.

Thompson, Leonard M. *Politics in the Republic of South Africa.* Boston: Little, Brown, 1966.

————. *The Unification of South Africa, 1902-1910.* Oxford: Clarendon Press, 1960.

van Jaarsveld, F. A. *The Awakening of Afrikaner Nationalism, 1868-1881.* Trans. P. R. Metrovich. Cape Town: Human and Rousseau, 1961.

van Rensburg, Hans. *Their Paths Crossed Mine: Memoirs of the Commandant-General of the Ossewa-Brandwag.* South Africa: Central News Agency, 1956.

Vatcher, William Henry, Jr. *White Laager: The Rise of Afrikaner Nationalism.* New York: Frederick A. Praeger, 1965.

Walker, Eric A. *A History of Southern Africa.* London: Longmans, Green, 1962.

Pamphlets

Hepple, Alex. *Trade Unions in Travail: The Story of the Broeder-Bond-Nationalist Plan to Control South African Trade Unions.* Johannesburg: Unity Publications, 1954.

Malherbe, E. G. *The Bilingual School.* Johannesburg: Central News Agency, 1943.

Rubin, Neville. *History of the Relations between NUSAS, the Afrikaanse Studentebond and the Afrikaans University Centers.* Cape Town: NUSAS, 1960.

Articles

In addition to the works cited below, the reader may wish to consult the regular coverage of South African affairs provided in *The Round Table: A Quarterly Review of British Commonwealth Affairs* (London, from 1910), *The Forum* (Johannesburg, weekly from April 4, 1938), and *New Nation* (Pretoria, monthly from August 1967).

Republic of South Africa. House of Assembly. *Index to the Manuscript Annexures and Printed Papers of the House of Assembly, including Select Committee Reports and Bills, and also to Principal Motions and Resolutions and Commission Reports, 1910-1960.* By order of Mr. Speaker, 1963.

Books

Adam, Heribert. *Modernizing Racial Domination: The Dynamics of South African Politics.* Berkeley: University of California Press, 1971.

Ballinger, Margaret. *From Union to Apartheid: A Trek to Isolation.* Cape Town: Juta, 1969.

Botha, Jan. *Verwoerd Is Dead.* Cape Town: Books of Africa, 1967.

Bunting, Brian. *The Rise of the South African Reich.* Harmondsworth: Penguin Books, 1964.

Carter, Gwendolen M. *The Politics of Inequality: South Africa Since 1948.* New York: Frederick A. Praeger, 1958.

Davenport, T. R. H. *The Afrikaner Bond: The History of a South African Political Party, 1880-1911.* Cape Town: Oxford University Press, 1966.

de Kiewiet, C. W. *A History of South Africa: Social and Economic.* London: Oxford University Press, 1966.

Hancock, W. K. *Smuts. Vol. I: The Sanguine Years. 1870-1919.* Cambridge: Cambridge University Press, 1962. *Smuts. Vol. II: The Fields of Force, 1919-1950.* Cambridge: Cambridge University Press, 1968.

Hepple, Alexander. *Verwoerd.* Harmondsworth: Penguin Books, 1967.

Karis, Thomas. "South Africa." In Gwendolen M. Carter (ed.), *Five African States: Responses to Diversity.* Ithaca: Cornell University Press, 1963, pp. 471-616.

Kruger, D. W. *The Age of the Generals: A Short Political History of the Union of South Africa, 1910-1948.* Johannesburg: Dagbreek Book Store, 1961.

———. (ed.). *South African Parties and Policies, 1910-1960: A Select Source Book.* Cape Town: Human & Rousseau, 1960.

Le May, G. M. *British Supremacy in South Africa.* London: Clarendon Press, 1965.

Lewin, Julius. *Politics and Law in South Africa.* London: Merlin Press, 1963.

Munger, Edwin S. *Afrikaner and African Nationalism: South African Parallels and Parameters.* London: Oxford University Press, 1967.

Brookes, Edgar H. "South Africa Swings Over." *Foreign Affairs,* XXVII, No. 1 (October 1948), 143-152.

―――. "The Union of South Africa: The General Election of 1958, and After." In Kenneth Kirkwood (ed.), *St. Anthony's Papers — Number 10.* London: Macmillan and Co., 1959, pp. 229-275.

Carter, Gwendolen M. "Union of South Africa: Politics of White Supremacy," *The Annals,* Vol. 298 (March 1955), 142-150.

de Villiers, Rene. "Afrikaner Nationalism." In Monica Wilson and Leonard Thompson (eds.), *Oxford History of South Africa,* Vol. II. New York and Oxford: Oxford University Press, 1971, pp. 365-423.

du Toit, Brian M. "Afrikaners, Nationalists and Apartheid," *Journal of Modern African Studies,* VIII, No. 4 (December 1970), 531-551.

―――. "Politics and Change in South Africa," *International Journal of Comparative Sociology,* VII (1966), 96-118.

―――. "Politics, Class and Caste in South Africa," *Journal of Asian and African Studies,* I, No. 3 (July 1966), 197-212.

Farguharson, R. R. "South Africa 1958." In D. E. Butler (ed.), *Elections Abroad.* London: Macmillan and Co., 1959, pp. 229-275.

Grey, J. L. "How the Nation Voted," *Common Sense,* August 1943.

Hancock, Sir Keith. "South African Elections," *Australian Journal of Science,* XXVIII, No. 3 (September 1965), 114-119.

Ilsley, Lucretia L. "The War Policy of South Africa," *American Political Science Review,* XXXIV, No. 6 (December 1940), 1178-1187.

Lever, H., and O. J. M. Wagner. "Urbanisation and the Afrikaner," *Race,* XI, No. 2 (October 1969), 183-188.

Longmore, L. "The Teenage Vote in South Africa," *Political Quarterly,* XXX, No. 2 (April-June 1959), 114-119.

Manning, Charles A. W. "In Defense of Apartheid," *Foreign Affairs,* XLIII, No. 1 (October 1964), 135-149.

Millin, Sarah Gertrude. "Smuts at Eighty," *Foreign Affairs,* XXIX, No. 1 (October 1950), 130-142.

Munger, Edwin S. "New White Politics in South Africa." In William A. Hance (ed.), *Southern Africa and the United States.* New York: Columbia University Press, 1968, pp. 33-84.

―――. "South Africa: Are There Silver Linings?" *Foreign Affairs,* XLVII, No. 2 (January 1969), 375-386.

O'Meara, Patrick. "Tensions in the Nationalist Party," *Africa Report,* XIV, No. 2 (February 1969), 24, 41-44.

Salomon, Larry. "The Economic Background to the Revival of Afrikaner Nationalism." In Jeffrey Butler (ed.), *Boston University Papers in African History,* Vol. I. Boston: Boston University Press, 1964, pp. 217-242.

Stadler, A. W. "The Afrikaner in Opposition, 1910-1948," *Journal of Commonwealth Political Studies,* VII, No. 3 (November 1969), 205-215.

Stultz, Newell M. "South African Cabinets and Ministers: Some Empirical Findings," *South Africa International,* III, No. 1 (July 1972), 1-18.

———. "The Politics of Security: South Africa Under Verwoerd, 1961-1966," *Journal of Modern African Studies,* VII, No. 1 (April 1969), 3-20.

———. "South Africa's 'Apartheid' Election of 1948 Reconsidered," *Plural Societies* (The Hague), III, No. 4 (Winter 1973), 25-38.

Stultz, Newell M., and Jeffrey Butler. "The South African General Election of 1961," *Political Science Quarterly,* LXXVIII, No. 1 (March 1963), 86-110.

Thompson, Leonard M. "Afrikaner Nationalist Historiography and the Policy of Apartheid," *Journal of African History,* III, No. 1 (1962), 125-141.

Tiryakian, Edward A. "Apartheid and Politics in South Africa," *Journal of Politics,* XXII, No. 4 (November 1960), 682-697.

Trapido, Stanley. "Political Institutions and Afrikaner Social Structure in the Republic of South Africa," *American Political Science Review,* LVII, No. 1 (March 1963), 75-87.

van den Berghe, Pierre L. "Albinocracy in South Africa: A Case Study in the Growth of Tyranny," *Journal of Asian and African Studies,* I, No. 1 (January 1966), 43-49.

Welsh, David. "Urbanisation and the Solidarity of Afrikaner Nationalism," *Journal of Modern African Studies,* VII, No. 2 (July 1969), 265-276.

Worrall, Denis. "Afrikaner Nationalism: A Contemporary Analysis." In Christian P. Potholm and Richard Dale (eds.), *Southern Africa in Perspective.* New York: The Free Press, 1971, pp. 19-30.

———. "Politics and Parties." In Denis Worrall (ed.), *South Africa: Government and Politics.* Pretoria: J. L. van Schaik, 1971, pp. 172-252.

———. "South Africa's 'Partition Election,' " *Africa Report,* XI, No. 5 (May 1966), 25-26.

Unpublished Theses

Briand-Kyrik, Florence R. "The Delimitation of Constituencies for the Union House of Assembly under the South Africa Act." M.A. dissertation, University of Cape Town, 1953.

Lovell, Colin Rhys. "Hertzog and the South African Nationalist Party." Ph.D. dissertation, University of Wisconsin, 1947.

Milnor, Andrew Johnson. "The Election of 1948 in the Union of South Africa, with Special Reference to the Origin and Development of the Reunited National Party." M.A. dissertation, Duke University, 1959.

Salomon, Laurence. "Socio-Economic Aspects of Modern South African History, 1870-1962." Ph.D. dissertation, Boston University, 1962.

Shaskolsky, Ralph. "An Examination of the Factors Leading Up to the H.N.P. Electoral Victory of 1948." B.A. (Hons.) extended essay, University of Cape Town, 1960.

Stultz, Newell M. "The Electoral Revival of the National Party in South Africa, 1934 to 1948." Ph.D. dissertation, Boston University, 1965.

Index